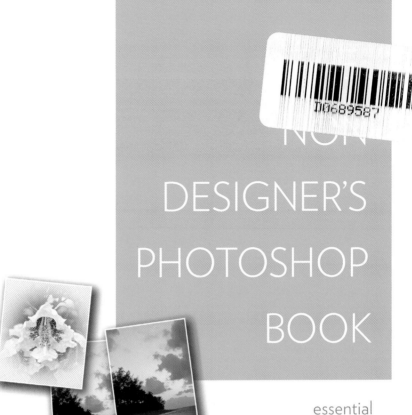

NON DESIGNER'S PHOTOSHOP BOOK

essential
imaging
techniques
for design

Robin Williams & John Tollett

Peachpit Press
Berkeley
California

The Non-Designer's Photoshop Book
ROBIN WILLIAMS AND JOHN TOLLETT

©2012 by Robin Williams and John Tollett

Peachpit Press
1249 Eighth Street
Berkeley, California 94710
510.524.2178   voice
510.524.2221   fax

Editor:	Nikki McDonald
Proofer:	Cathy Lane
Cover design and production:	John Tollett
Interior design:	Robin Williams
Production:	Robin Williams and John Tollett
Index:	Robin Williams
Prepress:	David Van Ness

Peachpit Press is a division of Pearson Education.

Find us on the web at www.peachpit.com.

To report errors, please send a note to errata@peachpit.com.

ISBN 13:   978-0-321-77283-1

ISBN 10:   0-321-77283-0

10 9 8 7 6 5 4 3 2 1

Printed and bound in the United States of America

Contents

3   Basic Technical Stuff

4   Select & Transform

5   All-Powerful Layers   91

6   Photoshop Type   115

7   Photoshop with a History   127

8 Adjustment Layers 133

9 Working with Transparency 149

10 Draw & Paint 155

11   Color Tools 185

12 Filters & Effects 193

13 Camera Raw 205

14 Puppet Warp 213

Index 217

READ THIS FIRST

Chances are you've used Photoshop on some level, but never had the time to become familiar with as many of the features and techniques as you would like. The first two chapters in this book get you up and running quickly while creating small projects from start to finish. The remaining chapters provide more exercises and detailed information for the types of tasks that are frequently encountered in graphic design (as opposed to photography).

Because Photoshop is an advanced application, we expect that you know how to use your mouse and the windows; the difference between a single click and a double click; how to find, open, and save files; how to access contextual menus (right-click or Control-click); and how to use your computer in general. But you probably know all those things already or you wouldn't be jumping into Photoshop!

This is not a manual, but more of an image-editing cookbook. Many of the steps and techniques you might need for various projects are littered throughout, so check the index for specific things you need.

We can't explain every single option in Photoshop (no one can do that in a book this small). The more you know about Photoshop the more you realize there are multiple ways to do almost anything. We hope that when you find a technique you like, it will spur you to go to Photoshop Help (from the Help menu) and find out more about it. As you explore the lessons in this book, we expect you to poke around, click and prod, and experiment. Turn the eyeball icons on and off and see what happens, rearrange layers, explore different Blending Modes, etc.

Of course, we're in awe of what this software can do because for many years we worked in the design world before Photoshop was invented. To you it might be just an ordinary, everyday miracle thingy. In any case, prepare to have more fun with software than you ever thought possible.

Things to know before you begin

Right-click: Because most people these days have a two-button mouse, we use the phrase "right-click" to mean "right-click *or* if you don't have a two-button mouse on a Mac, Control-click."

We use the terms **press** and **drag**. *Press* means to hold down the mouse and don't release it until you finish the current instruction. *Drag* means to press on the mouse, then drag the cursor without releasing the mouse until you've completed the drag operation. We avoid the term "click-and-drag" because for many things, if you click (which implies you let go), the drag won't work.

To keep text short and easy to understand, most instructions for **choosing menu items** are in this form: From the Layer menu, choose New > Layer via Copy. This means go to the Layer menu, slide down to "New," and from its submenu, choose "Layer via Copy."

Brushes: Many tools have brush-like qualities but you don't think of them as brushes. See pages 170–175 for controlling the paint brushes and know that the same techniques control other "brushes" such as the Eraser tool, Quick Selection tool, Clone Stamp tool, Blur tool, etc. Get in the habit of using the [and] keys to reduce and enlarge the size of the brushes as you work.

Choose your tool, then check the Options bar to see what its settings are! That's one of the biggest causes of frustration—not realizing that there is some setting that is messing up your expectations. Photoshop does exactly what you tell it—it's *your* job to understand what you're telling it!

Check the **Cursors** preferences (page 171) so you understand that you have control over how it appears.

Learn your keyboard shortcuts. We often tell you to go to a menu and choose a command, but when you go to the menu, also take note of and learn the shortcut.

One that Photoshopped not wisely but too well

Almost Famous Quotes
from Non-Designer
Shakespeare

Photoshop: It's like a recipe for creativity.

1 The Photoshop Interface

If you're at least vaguely familiar with Adobe InDesign or Illustrator, the Photoshop interface should look familiar in many ways. The following pages provide an overview of the essential windows, panels, and icons that come into play for almost every Photoshop task or project.

In this chapter we've labeled many of the buttons and icons that are mentioned in the step-by-step exercises. If you can't find something, come back to this chapter and look for it (or check the index).

In addition to an overview of the main interface, we describe many of the options and preferences you should be aware of so you can understand and take advantage of this truly amazing software.

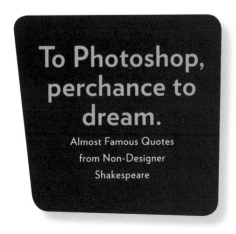

To Photoshop, perchance to dream.

Almost Famous Quotes
from Non-Designer
Shakespeare

Photoshop interface overview

Brush Preset picker.

Tabbed document windows. **To separate the windows,** *go to the Window menu and choose Arrange > Float All in Windows.*

Application bar. *Hide or show it from the Window menu.*

Options bar.
The options you see in this bar are dependent on which tool is selected—choose a different tool, see different options.

Tools panel.
*Tools with small **triangles** in the bottom-right corners have additional tools hidden in the same space. **Press** on a tool to reveal a pop-out menu that displays the hidden tools.*

Foreground *and* **Background** *color boxes.*

Quick Mask Mode.

To show rulers, *choose View > Show Rulers.* **To hide rulers,** *choose View > Hide Rulers.*

Status bar/document information.

2

The current document name is displayed here, and its tab is white.

Workspace switcher. *This is only visible when the Application bar is showing; otherwise use the Window > Workspace menu.*

The **Collapse To Icons** button (double arrows). Click to **toggle** between panel icons and expanded panels.

Layers panel icon.

When panels are **docked,** as shown here, they expand one at a time, keeping the workspace uncluttered.

Panels that are docked as a group expand together. As **shown** expanded, the Layers, Adjustments, and History panels are a group.

To expand a panel, single-click its icon.

To collapse back to icons in the vertical dock, single-click the double triangles in the panel title bar.

To dock panels in other arrangements, drag the icons into another group.

To float a panel anywhere, drag it away from the dock.

Panels minimized to icon mode in a vertical dock. **To expand the dock** to show panel names, drag the left side of the dock toward the center of the window.

Panels overview

Panels provide tools, such as the Tools panel on the left side of the screen, and other specific tool options and controls in the panels stacked in the vertical dock on the right side of the screen. The following tips are to help you understand and manage panels.

- Panels have a panel menu (circled, right). Click it to show a pop-up menu of useful options and commands.

- When several panels are stacked in a panel **group**, as shown here, each panel is identified with a tab. **To separate a panel from the others**, drag its tab out of the panel group and float it anywhere on the Desktop.

- **To minimize a floating panel**, click the double arrow icon in the top-right corner.

- **To expand panels** (docked or floating) to display both panel icon and panel label, drag one side of the panel away from the center, shown on the right.

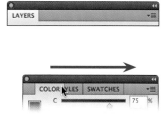

- **To minimize a panel** and show only the tab, double-click the tab or the gray title bar. **To expand the panel**, double-click the tab or gray title bar area again.

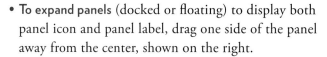

- **To rearrange the tabs in a panel group**, drag a tab left or right.

- **To rearrange panels in a vertical dock** (shown to the right), drag a panel to another position in the dock. A blue drop zone indicates where the panel will be placed when you release.

- **To add a panel to the dock**, select it from the Window menu, then dock it where you want.

- **To remove a panel from the dock, and close it**, right-click its tab, then choose "Close."

TIP: To hide or show all open panels in any screen mode, tap the Tab key.

Control your panels

To display a default set of panels, shown below left, click "Essentials" in the workspace switcher area in the Applications bar (see it on page 3).

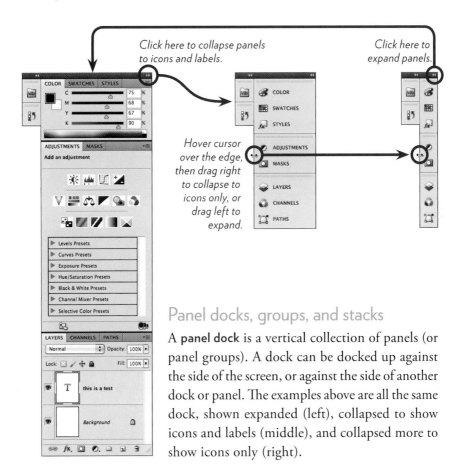

Click here to collapse panels to icons and labels.

Click here to expand panels.

Hover cursor over the edge, then drag right to collapse to icons only, or drag left to expand.

Panel docks, groups, and stacks

A **panel dock** is a vertical collection of panels (or panel groups). A dock can be docked up against the side of the screen, or against the side of another dock or panel. The examples above are all the same dock, shown expanded (left), collapsed to show icons and labels (middle), and collapsed more to show icons only (right).

- **To dock a panel**, drag it into the dock. Release the drag when a blue drop zone appears where you want to position the panel.

- **To dock a panel group**, drag it by its title bar (the solid empty bar above the tabs) into the dock.

- **To remove a panel or panel group from a dock**, drag it out of the dock by its tab or title bar. Drag it into another dock or float it anywhere in the workspace.

A **panel stack** is a group of floating, minimized panels that move together when you drag it by the topmost title bar. **To minimize a panel**, double-click its tab.

- **To stack floating panels,** drag a minimized panel's tab to the blue drop zone (that appears when your cursor is over a drop zone) at the bottom of another panel or panel group.

- **To change the stacking order of panels,** drag a panel up or down by its tab. Release the tab over the narrow drop zone *between* panels, rather than the drop zone in a title bar.

- **To remove a panel** (or panel group) from the stack, drag it out by its tab or title bar.

This stack is made of three panel groups.

A **panel group** is a collection of panels grouped together as tabs under the same title bar (the empty gray bar above panel tabs). You can create a group of frequently used panels, or create groups of any kind that help your workflow.

- **To move a panel into a group,** drag the panel's tab to the highlighted drop zone in the group.

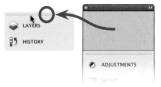

To disengage a panel group from a dock, *press on its finger grip (the double dotted lines) and drag the panel group out of the dock. Or drag a panel tab out of a tabbed group (below, right).*

Four views of the same panel group.

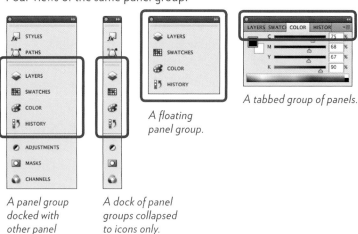

A panel group docked with other panel groups.

A dock of panel groups collapsed to icons only.

A floating panel group.

A tabbed group of panels.

Workspace overview

Once you get all your favorite panels in the groups and docks and positions you like best, you can save that arrangement so that with the click of a button they'll all be in their correct places whenever you need them. The workspace switcher lets you switch between the various layouts you might need for different projects. Adobe has already created some workspaces for you (Design, Painting, Photography, etc.), but you can also create your own, save them in the workspace switcher, and use them again for future projects.

1　Arrange the panels as you want them.

2　Click the double arrows in the workspace switcher section of the Application bar, shown below. From the menu that appears, choose "New Workspace… ."

Or from the Window menu, choose Workspace > New Workspace….

Workspace choices.

Click here to see more workspaces and other options.

3　In the "New Workspace" dialog that opens, type a name for the new workspace.

4　Name the workspace, and then click "Save."

To delete a custom workspace, choose "Delete Workspace…" from the workspace switcher menu (shown above) *or* from Window > Workspace. Choose your workspace and click "Delete."

To reset a workspace if things have moved around, from the Window menu, choose Workspace > Reset *Workspace Name*.

Screen modes

There are three different screen view modes: standard, full screen with menu bar, and full screen. **To change screen modes**, tap the **F** key. Subsequent taps cycle through all screen modes. (Make sure a text box is not active, or you'll just type the letter "f" instead of changing screen modes.)

Tools overview

The tools in the Tools panel are grouped into categories, as shown to the right.

To change the Tools panel to a two-column panel, as shown below-left, single-click the double arrow button in its top-right corner. **To switch back to column panel,** click the double-arrow button again.

To float the Tools panel anywhere on the Desktop, drag it away from the screen edge.

To dock it to the edge of the screen, drag the panel all the way to the edge until a blue vertical bar appears against the edge of the screen. This is a visual clue that the panel is docked. Let go and the panel snaps in place.

All tools except the top and bottom ones (the Move tool and the Zoom tool) have small triangles in the bottom-right corner, indicating hidden tools in the same space. **To reveal a menu of hidden tools,** *press* (don't click) or right-click on one of these tools (see below). The hidden tools are closely related in function to the tool they hide under.

To quickly cycle through hidden tools, hold down the Shift key and tap the tool's keyboard shortcut that appears in tool tips (see next page).

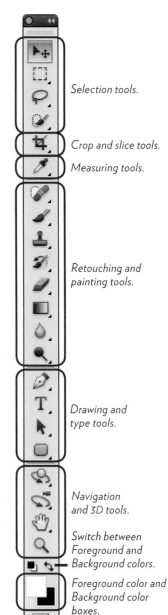

Selection tools.

Crop and slice tools.

Measuring tools.

Retouching and painting tools.

Drawing and type tools.

Navigation and 3D tools.

Switch between Foreground and Background colors.

Foreground color and Background color boxes.

Quick Mask mode.

A two-column view of the Tools panel. Single-click the double-arrow icon (or double-click anywhere in the top bar) to switch between one and two-column views.

Press on a tool in the Tools panel to show hidden tools.

Most tools and icons have hidden **tool tips** that appear when you hover the cursor over the item. Use this feature when you've forgotten what a certain tool looks like, which icon you need to choose, or just to tell you what it is.

The **letter in a Tool tool tip** indicates which key to press to select that tool. Some tools have the same letter key, such as the Brush, Pencil, and two other tools in the same slot. Hold down the Shift key and tap the letter key to cycle through all tools with that letter key.

If tool tips don't appear, turn them on in Preferences: From the Photoshop menu (PC: Edit menu), choose Preferences > Interface…, then put a check in the "Show Tool Tips" box.

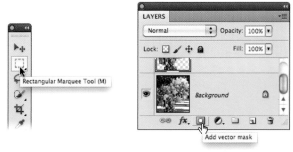

Hover the cursor over a tool or icon to display a descriptive tool tip.

Panels, dialogs, and items in the Options bar often have fields that require a value, such as the Opacity options in the Layers panel, shown below. **To enter a value** in a field do one of the following:

- Type a value in the field.

- Single-click the blue triangle next to the field to display a slider (below, left). Drag the slider button left or right.

- Position the cursor over the title of the field (below, right). When the cursor changes to a pointing finger, drag left or right. This is called a *scrubby slider*. **To change the increments by a factor of ten**, hold down the Shift key.

 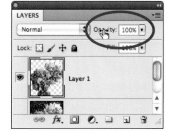

Rulers and the Ruler tool

Rulers are extremely useful for positioning image elements and guide lines—and even more useful if you know a couple of tips for manipulating them.

- **To show or hide rulers**, from the View menu, choose "Rulers."

- **To change the ruler's unit of measurement**, right-click a ruler (the horizontal or vertical one) to show a pop-up menu of options, then select one (below, left).

- **To change the zero origin**, the point at which the ruler begins measurement, press in the top-left corner and drag to the spot where you want the zero position to start (above, right).

- **To reset the zero origin** to its original position, double-click the top left corner where the two rulers meet.

Measure a distance or straighten a photo

In addition to the rulers, you can use the Ruler tool to measure lengths, place elements exact distances apart, and even to straighten photos. The Ruler tool is hidden under the Eyedropper tool (see page 8 to access it).

- **Measure a length:** Select the Ruler tool, then drag across the image from one point to another. A non-printing line appears and the measurement information appears in the Options bar. Drag the measurement line to another position to use it as a spacing guide.
  Reposition the line: Press on the line's middle section and drag.
  Resize the line: Drag one of its end points.
  Remove the ruler line: Click the "Clear" button in the Options bar.

- **Straighten a photo:** Select the Ruler tool, drag along the edge of an element in the image that should be perfectly horizontal or vertical, then click the *Straighten* button in the Options bar.

Document guides

Guides are helpful when you need to align objects or text. Make sure the rulers are showing: press Command R (PC: Control R).

- **Place a guide on the image:** Press on a ruler and drag a guide out of the ruler and into the image. Let go to drop the guide wherever you want it.

- **Reposition a guide:** Select the Move tool in the Tools panel. Press on an existing guide and drag it to a new position.

- **Clear guides:** From the View menu, choose "Clear Guides."

- **Lock guides** so you don't accidentally move them: From the View menu, choose "Lock Guides."

- **Hide or show existing guides:** From the View menu, choose Show > Guides.

- **Turn on Smart Guides:** From the View menu, choose Show > Smart Guides. Smart Guides automatically appear when you move an element near another object that you might want to align it to.

- **Make elements snap to guides:** From the View menu, choose "Snap." **Specify which elements to snap to:** From the View menu, choose "Snap To," then choose one of the options (guides, grid, layer content, slice boundaries, document edges, all, or none).

Zoom in or out

Zoom is a great and versatile feature. Open an image and practice these techniques so they become comfortable and automatic to use.

- **To magnify the view:** Press Command + (PC: Control +) (that's the *plus sign* in the upper-right of your keyboard).

- **To reduce the view:** Press Command – (PC: Control –) (that's the *minus sign* to the left of the plus sign).

- **To magnify or reduce the view:** Hold down Command Spacebar (PC: Control Spacebar) and drag left or right anywhere in the image.

- **To magnify or reduce the view:** Select the Zoom tool and single-click in the image to magnify it. Hold down the Option key (PC: Alt key), which makes the plus sign in the Zoom tool become a minus sign— click in the image with the minus Zoom tool to reduce the view.

—continued

- **To snap to a view size of 100 percent:** Double-click the Zoom tool in the Tools panel. *Or* from the View menu, choose "Actual Pixels." *Or* press Command 0 (PC: Control 0)—that's the *zero* in the row of numbers across the top of your keyboard.

- **To view an exact percentage size:** Change the percentage value in the bottom-left corner of the document window, then press the Enter key. You can also click in that little field and use the up and down arrows to change the percentage; hit the Enter key to activate the change.

- **To fit an image on the screen as large as possible:** Double-click the Hand tool in the Tools panel.

- **To view another area of an enlarged image:** To practice, first enlarge the image so big that it is not all visible in the window, or make the window smaller. Now hold down the H key, then press-and-hold the mouse button. While the H key is held down, a marquee in the shape of the current window is visible. Continue holding down the H key and drag the marquee to an area of the image you want displayed. When you release the H key, that section of the image returns to the previous magnification. Try it.

- **To magnify a specific part of an image:** Select the Zoom tool, then press-and-drag with it over the area you want to zoom into.

- **To zoom in continuously:** Position the Zoom tool on the image, then press the mouse button while the image magnifies.

- **To zoom out continuously:** Hold the Option (PC: Alt) key as you press the mouse button, as above.

Pixel grid

When the image preview is higher than 500 percent magnification, a pixel grid is visible, as shown below. **To hide the white lines of this grid**, from the View menu, choose "Show," then deselect the "Pixel Grid" option.
Of course you can always choose to show it when you decide you want to see the individual pixels.

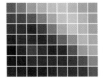

The pixel grid can be useful when you need to do really close and detailed work.

2 Simple Projects

The seemingly endless list of things you can do in Photoshop can be intimidating and might prevent some non-designers (and designers) from jumping in to learn the program. If that sounds like you, don't worry—you're in good company.

Much of what we learned about Photoshop happened gradually, learning what we needed at the moment to do a certain task. But we want you to learn the same things quickly, instead of waiting for specific situations to show up in real world projects— which could take years… aaarrgh! One thing you can be very happy about is the fact that every version of Photoshop gets more powerful *and* easier. Some operations that used to be complex and weird can now be accomplished with a click or two. *That's* the kind of technical expertise we love.

This chapter includes a collection of common image-editing tasks you're likely to encounter and will introduce you to many of the features and techniques in Photoshop. Follow along with these tasks on your own photos to familiarize yourself with commands you'll use every day in other projects.

If you're not very familiar with the Photoshop interface, go back to Chapter 1 at any time for an overview of where things are and what they're called.

Almost every task in Photoshop requires you to check the controls in the Options bar, so get in the habit of choosing a tool and checking the Options bar to see what the settings are.

Whiten teeth

If only it was this quick and easy in real life. Hopefully, you won't have a more challenging teeth-whitening client than this one. If there's not a lot of discoloration and you just want to quickly lighten the teeth, skip to Step 4.

1   Open an image of someone with less than perfectly white teeth.

 2   Select the Sponge tool, hidden under the Dodge tool (shown on the right).
In the Options bar, set "Mode" to *Desaturate* and "Flow" to *100%*.

Select a brush size *for the Sponge that makes it easy to brush just the teeth:*

For a **smaller** *brush, tap the left bracket key.*

For a **larger** *brush, tap the right bracket key.*

3   Scrub the teeth with the Sponge tool to remove color from the teeth.

 4   Now select the Dodge tool.
In the Options bar, set the "Range" to *Highlights* and set "Exposure" to *20%*.

6   Scrub the teeth with the Dodge tool.

Reset the "Range" to *Midtones,* then scrub the teeth again.

Finally, reset the "Range" to *Shadows* and finish scrubbing the teeth.

As you work, be careful not to scrub away detail or make teeth so white that it looks unnatural, like the blinding glare of movie-star teeth.

Remove dust and scratches

Scanned images, such as old family photos, often show dust and scratches. The dust is sometimes on the scanner glass, not the photo, so Step 1 should be "clean the scanner glass surface before you scan." If your photo shows dust specs, scratches, or blemishes of almost any kind on the subject or background, the Spot Healing Brush is a quick and easy miracle tool.

1 Open an image that has dust or scratches.

2 From the Tools panel, select the Spot Healing Brush tool.

3 In the Options bar (shown below), select "Content-Aware." Brush over the areas you want to repair, as explained below.

   There's a filter for dust and scratches. But it blurs the image to do the job, usually too much blur, so we prefer this method.

Brush Preset picker.

When you select the Spot Healing Brush it appears here, in the Tool Preset picker.

For small specks and blemishes, just tap the tool on the spot to remove it.

For long scratches, drag the Spot Healing Brush across them. As you drag, the brush appears to paint a black stroke (shown, left), but when you stop the stroke, the repaired result appears. (If you don't like it, Undo.)

When painting close to an edge, such as between the white collar and the black jacket shown here, use a hard brush: Single-click on the Brush Preset picker (shown above) and set the *Hardness* slider to 100%. When the brush is not near an edge, a softer brush (a lower percentage) works well.

Correct a photo that's too light

Give new life to faded photo memories with a simple adjustment.

1 Open an overexposed or faded image.

The original, faded photo.

2 From the Image menu, choose Adjustments > Levels… .

3 In the Levels panel, drag the black triangle under the histogram (the spiky image) to the *right* until it aligns with the left edge of the histogram (as shown below, right). Drag the white triangle to the *left* to align it with the right side of the histogram. Click OK.

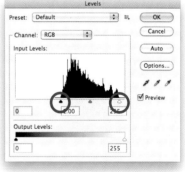

Correct contrast with one click

The problem with this image is similar to that on the opposite page—flat, with a lack of contrast. This time, however, we're going to let Photoshop do all the work because dragging sliders and triangles is too tiring.

1 Open an image that has poor contrast.

2 From the Layer menu, choose New Adjustment Layer > Levels; click OK.

3 In the Levels panel that appears (you might have to hunt for it if you've got a lot of panels open), click the "Auto" button (circled below, right).

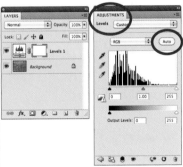

Rescue photos that are too dark

Even a seemingly worthless photo like this one contains lots of digital information and detail that can be brought out from the dark.

1 Open an image that's underexposed or too dark.

2 From the Image menu, choose Adjustments > Shadows/Highlights... to open the "Shadows/Highlights" panel (below, right). The "Shadows" *Amount* slider is set to 35% by default, which is usually too much for most images. Drag the slider back to the left, to about 10%, but don't let the dark tones don't get too washed out.

3 To enrich the color a bit, move the "Color Correction" slider to +50 (or whatever works best for your image). Click OK.

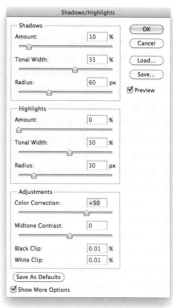

Make wrinkles disappear

Some of us would like the Spot Healing Brush tool in our makeup bags.

1 Select the Spot Healing Brush tool.

2 In the Options bar (shown below): Select a brush size and hardness from the Brush Preset picker; choose a brush *Size* slightly larger than the wrinkles you want to remove, and set the *Hardness* to 0%.

To change brush sizes on the fly, tap the left bracket key [to *reduce* brush size, and tap the right bracket key] to *increase* brush size.

Brush Preset picker.

3 In the Options bar, above, set the "Type" to *Content-Aware*.

4 Press-and-drag the brush across wrinkles (below left) to blend them with the skin color and texture.

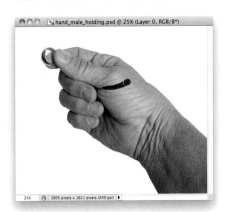
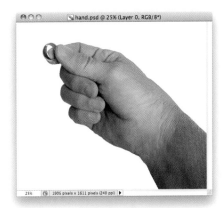

5 To add more smoothness: From the Filter menu, choose Blur > Surface Blur…. Surface Blur ignores edges, more or less, depending on your settings. In the "Surface Blur" dialog (right), adjust the *Radius* and *Threshold* settings to your satisfaction.

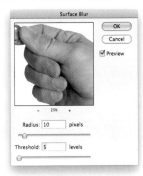

The Surface Blur filter is also useful for minimizing unwanted noise and texture.

TIP: Press on the Surface Blur dialog preview to see the original image inside the pane; release to see the filtered effect. To toggle between before and after views in the document window, check/uncheck the Preview box, or tap the P key.

Convert a color photo to black and white

Photoshop can automatically convert color images to grayscale: From the Image menu, choose Mode > Grayscale. But this doesn't give you any control over the conversion. When you convert a photo to black and white, you can use an Adjustment Layer so you can control the final appearance of the image.

1 Open a color image.

2 Create a new Adjustment Layer: From the Layers menu, choose New Adjustment Layer > Black & White. Click OK.

3 In the Adjustments panel that appears, drag the color sliders to lighten or darken the grayscale conversion for that color.

Doing this on an Adjustment Layer allows you to change the grayscale appearance later, if need be.

Original color image.

An automatic grayscale conversion.

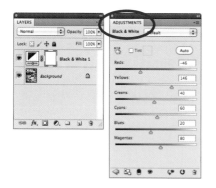

This controlled grayscale conversion has more contrast.

Fix blown-out whites

This technique works best on photos that were shot in the *raw* format. Raw is an uncompressed format that retains invisible digital image information that Photoshop can recover, as opposed to JPEGs that are compressed.

1 Open an image file that includes white areas.

From the Image menu, choose Adjustments > Shadows/Highlights….

2 In the "Shadows/Highlights" panel (below right), set the "Shadows" *Amount* slider to *0%*.

Set the "Highlights" *Amount* slider to the right to darken the highlights, but don't make them too dark.

3 Drag the "Highlights" *Tonal Width* and *Radius* sliders left or right until you're satisfied with the results. Click OK.

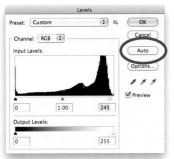

If the image appears too dark, go to the Image menu and choose Adjustments > Levels…. Click the "Auto" button. *Or* drag the highlights slider (the white triangle under the histogram) to the left.

Alter colors with ease

Of the many ways to adjust colors, this is one of the easiest and quickest.

1 Open an image you want to adjust.

2 Create a new Adjustment Layer: If the Adjustments panel is not open on your screen, go to the Window menu and choose "Adjustments." (If there is a checkmark next to its name, that means it is already open.)

In the Adjustments panel, click the *Hue/Saturation* icon (circled below). This creates the new layer in the Layers panel and opens the *Hue/Saturation* panel.

3 In the *Hue/Saturation* pane, select the *Targeted Adjustment* tool (circled, right).

4 Click on a color in the image that you want to adjust.

Now hold down the Command key (PC: Control key) and drag left or right in the image (below).

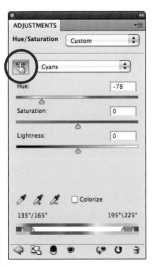

The Targeted Adjustment tool samples the range of colors at the point of the click. When you hold down the Command (or Control) key, the **Hue** slider automatically moves left and right as you drag the cursor left and right, and changes the hue of the sampled color range, wherever it occurs in the image.

If you drag the cursor *without* a key held down, it adjusts the **Saturation** of the sampled color. Experiment with both possibilities and combinations.

Alter colors in Camera Raw

This is a quick introduction to the Camera Raw work area. There's more information about Camera Raw in Chapter 13, but this example quickly demonstrates how easily you can alter entire color ranges in images, even if they were not shot in the raw format to begin with.

1 From the File menu, choose Open....

2 In the Open dialog, single-click to select a JPEG image.

3 From the "Format" pop-up menu, choose "Camera Raw."

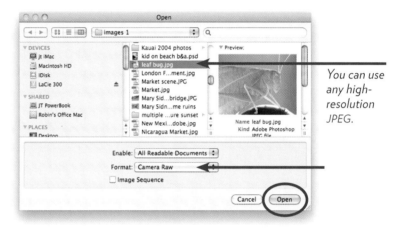

You can use any high-resolution JPEG.

4 Click "Open." The image opens in the Camera Raw interface, as shown below.

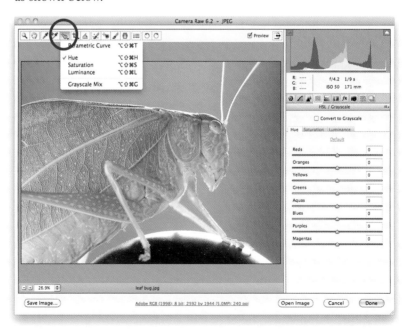

5   Press (don't click) on the *Targeted Adjustment* tool icon in the tool bar, circled on the previous page, to display a menu of options. Choose *Hue*.

6   The Targeted Adjustment tool samples the color range at the point where you click in the image, and the cursor changes to a horizontal double-arrow. Single-click on a color in the image, then drag the cursor horizontally left or right to change the hue of that color range.

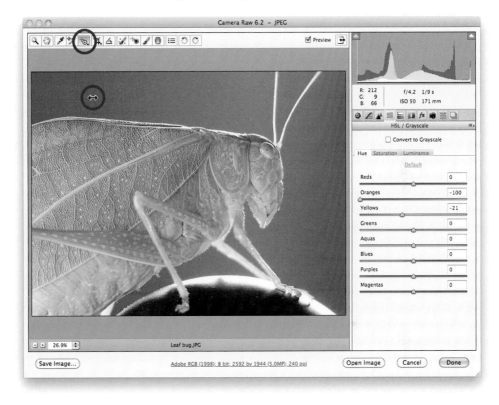

If you were to click with the Targeted Adjustment tool in the green body of the bug, greens would be sampled and then altered as you drag left or right.

To alter the image saturation, luminance, or grayscale settings, press on the Targeted Adjustment tool again to reveal the pop-up menu shown on the opposite page. Make your choice and follow the steps as above.

To revert to the original appearance after experimenting with the Camera Raw tools and settings, but still carry on experimenting, hold down the Option key (PC: Alt key). The "Cancel" button changes to "Reset." With the Option or Alt key held down, click the "Reset" button and carry on.

Straighten a photo

Straightening a photo can't get much easier than this.

1 Open an image that you want straightened.

2 Select the **Ruler tool**. It is stored under the Eyedropper in the Tools panel—press or right-click on the Eyedropper to reveal a pop-up menu that contains the Ruler tool; select the Ruler tool.

3 Drag the Ruler tool along an edge or shape in the photo that you want to straighten. (The image is faded here to make the Ruler's path more visible. In reality, when you drag the Ruler tool, the image is unchanged.)

4 Click the "Straighten" button in the Options bar (shown below).

To start over with the Ruler tool, click the "Clear" button instead of "Straighten."

5 If the final result crops away too much of the image, press Command Z (PC: Control Z) which will undo the crop and enlarge the document window to show the entire straightened image.

Since this image we're using started as a closely cropped image, the background must necessarily be radically cropped. Fortunately, there is Photoshop magic available to reconstruct the background, as shown on the following page.

Fill a background

Content-Aware Fill analyzes the image and attempts to fill a selected area with content that matches the existing background. It works better on some images than others. Images may need various degrees of touch-up after applying this feature.

 1 Choose the **Quick Selection tool** from the Tools panel.

2 Click in each area of white space that you need to fill; the click with the Quick Selection tool will select the contiguous (touching) white space.

3 From the Edit menu, choose "Fill...."

In the "Fill" dialog that opens, set the "Use" pop-up menu to "Content-Aware."

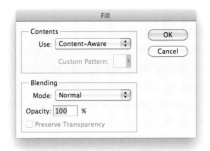

4 Click OK. The fill (shown middle-right) is not perfect, but amazing nonetheless.

In this example, if the top edge and right corner aren't needed, the image could be cropped and would look fine. But if the entire image is needed, then some touch-up with the Clone Stamp tool can finish the job, as shown to the right.

Learn about the Stamp Clone tool on pages 58.

Remove electrical power lines

Because power lines are everywhere, it's almost impossible to keep them out of photos, at least in urban areas. You can use the same Spot Healing Brush that we used on page 19 to eliminate power lines as easily as wrinkles, or the Clone Stamp tool, page 58. But if you're familiar with using the Pen tool to draw a path, here's a technique that's more accurate. (If you're not familiar with the Pen tool, see pages 160–63.)

1 Open an image in which you need to remove the power lines.

2 Open the Paths panel. From the panel menu that pops out when you click the top-right corner (below, left), choose "New Path…." Name the path, if you want, then click OK.

 3 Select the Pen tool from the Tools panel. Draw a path on top of one of the power lines in the photo.

This is the path.

 4 With the new path layer in the Paths panel selected (highlighted in blue, as shown in Step 2, above), select the Spot Healing Brush tool from the Tools panel.

5 In the Options bar, click the Brush Preset picker (shown below). Choose a brush *Size* slightly thicker than the power line, and set the brush *Hardness* to 0% (a soft-edged brush).

6 Also in the Options bar, check the button to set "Proximity Match."

Brush Preset picker

7 Select the *Stroke Path* icon (circled below, left), located at the bottom of the Paths panel. A black Spot Healing Brush stroke appears on top of the path (below right), and a small progress wheel indicator spins while Photoshop analyzes the image.

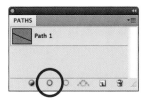

After a few anxious moments of anticipation, the black brush stroke disappears.

To remove the path and reveal a nicely retouched sky, press Delete (PC: Backspace).

Repeat this operation for each power line.

Alternatively: Draw all the paths, set the Spot Healing Brush parameters, then click the *Stroke Path* icon at the bottom of the Paths panel.

This technique also works great for taking airplane contrails out of the skies of your otherwise perfect landscape shots.

Liven up a dull exposure

At first glance, the photo below looks like a nice, colorful image. But if you look with a more critical eye, the contrast is flat and the colors are rather dull. Keep in mind that our digital cameras, amazing as they may be, are imperfect and limited in their ability to capture reality in all its glory. In other words, don't be timid about juicing up a photo to make it match what you saw with your own beady eyes.

The contrast in this image is flat.

1 Open a dull image that needs to be enriched.

2 To adjust the contrast, do one or both of the following:

- From the Image menu, choose "Auto Contrast."
  This option doesn't give you any control over the results, but it can work very well.

- From the Image menu, choose Adjustments > Levels…, then click the "Auto" button in the Levels dialog.

For many images, this is all you'll need to do. To explore more options for adjustments to the contrast, continue to the following page.

Manually adjust the contrast

From the Image menu, choose Adjustments > Levels…, then drag the triangles located under the Histogram (shown below).

As a general rule, drag the black triangle to the *right* until it aligns with the left side of the histogram, and drag the white triangle to the *left* until it aligns with the right side of the histogram. You should, however, use your own visual judgment to decide how much adjustment to make.

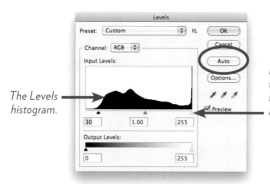

The Levels histogram.

Drag these sliders to adjust the **shadows** (the black triangle), the **midtones** (the gray triangle), and the **highlights** (the white triangle).

More contrast makes a big difference, but if the colors are still too dull, from the Image menu, choose Adjustments > Vibrance…. The Vibrance dialog has adjustment sliders for both *Vibrance* and *Saturation*. The *Vibrance* setting saturates colors that are under-represented, and it mostly ignores skin tones. The *Saturation* setting saturates all colors.

Resize a photo without cropping

Imagine that a brochure layout has space for a photo, but the photo is quite a bit wider than the space allotted. The client doesn't want to crop out any of the people or make the photo any smaller, horizontally or vertically, than the space allotted in the design. Sounds impossible, but not if you use Content-Aware Scale. This feature analyzes an image and attempts to scale it by affecting areas that don't contain important visual elements. If the image is a landscape without unusual elements, skip Steps 2 and 3. But if you need to ensure you don't lose anything important, first preserve specific areas of an image using an *alpha channel,* as shown here.

1   Open an image that you wish was more compact in composition.

2   Select the Lasso tool in the Tools panel.

Draw paths around the areas you want to preserve (just press and drag). **To make multiple selections**, as shown below, create the first selection, then hold down the Shift key to draw subsequent selections that will be added to the first (you'll see a small plus sign next to the Lasso brush when it's adding).

Since we're going to reduce only the width of this sample photo, we made sure that a generous amount of the image width is *not* preserved so Photoshop has plenty of unimportant pixels to delete without messing too much with the pixels we want to preserve.

3   Choose "Channels" from the Window menu to open the Channels panel. Make sure the areas in your image are still selected, then click the *Save Selection as Channel* button (circled below).

This alpha channel gets automatically created when you click the button (Save Selection as Channel).

4   If you're scaling a Background layer (and we are), go to the Select menu and choose "All." If we had duplicated the Background layer and worked on the duplicate, this step would be optional.

5   From the Edit menu, choose "Content-Aware Scale." This puts a marquee with handles around your image. Drag one of the side handles of the marquee in toward the center a bit to scale the width. Switch to the other side of the image and drag that side in toward the center. If you drag too far you'll see unwanted distortion, as shown on the right. Hey wait, that looks kinda cool!

6   Hit the Enter key to commit the transformation. If you prefer to click a button, the *Cancel Transform* and *Commit Transform* icons are available in the Options bar.

Extend a photo

When you need just a little extra sky or horizon or foreground, you can use Free Transform to stretch the dimensions of a photo. Obviously this works best on sky or horizons that don't contain detail that will look distorted when you stretch it.

1   Open an image file.
    From the Image menu, choose "Canvas Size…."

2   In the "Canvas Size" panel (below), change the width or height measurement to the size you want your photo to occupy. For this example, we changed the width from 8 inches to 9.5 inches.

3   Choose the *Anchor* position. The gray square indicates where the existing image will be positioned, or anchored, as extra canvas is added to the document. The arrows point where new canvas can go. Simply click in any square to make that the anchor point.

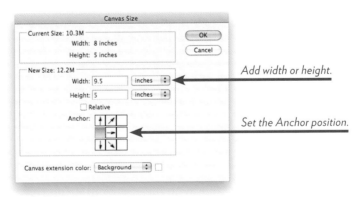

Add width or height.

Set the Anchor position.

4   Select the Rectangular Marquee tool. Drag a selection around the side of the image that you want to extend (shown below).

5   From the Edit menu, choose "Free Transform." This creates a marquee and control handles around the selection.

6   Drag the outside handle to the edge to fill the blank canvas area. Hit Enter to commit to the transformation.
    From the Select menu, choose "Deselect" to hide the marquee.

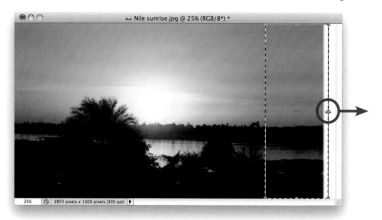

Extra image can be added vertically in the same way, as shown below.

1   In the "Canvas Size" panel, add canvas to the top of the image.

2   Create a rectangular selection across the sky.

3   Follow steps 5 and 6, above.

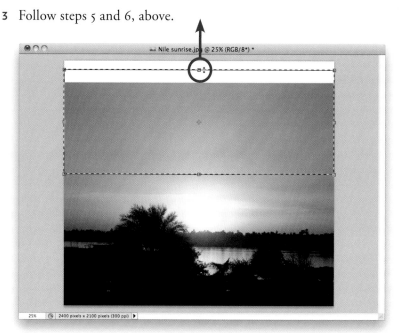

Blur a background instead of replacing it

You need a portrait-style shot, but all you have is a candid snapshot. You can transform a snapshot like this into a portrait by blurring the background beyond recognition.

1   Open an image that contains a potentially nice portrait shot.

2   Select the Quick Selection tool in the Tools panel. Drag inside the subject to make a quick, rough selection, as shown below. (This tool detects edges and selects up to them; if your subject's clothes or hair blend into the background, you might need to use the technique on pages 55–57.)

Click the eyeball icon to turn off a layer's visibility.

3   From the Layer menu, choose New > Layer via Copy. A new layer containing the selection appears in the Layers panel (above right). Click the eyeball to turn off the *Background* layer visibility.

4   To erase parts of the background that remain on this layer, select the Eraser tool in the Tools panel.
    In the Brush Preset picker, set the *Hardness* to around 50%.
    To adjust the Eraser size as needed, tap the left or right bracket keys.
    Drag the Eraser over the areas that need to be cleaned up.

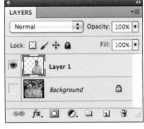

5   In the Layers panel, turn on the visibility of the *Background* so you can blur it: Click in the empty spot where its eyeball icon should be.

Select the *Background* layer: Single-click on its name.

6   Blur the Background copy: From the Filter menu, choose Blur > Gaussian Blur....

In the "Gaussian Blur" dialog, drag the *Radius* slider to the right until you're satisfied with the blur effect. Click OK.

The background now looks a lot like a portrait studio background.

7   For a final touch-up, if necessary, you might want to soften the edges of the foreground subject so it doesn't stand out harshly against the blurred background.

• Select the Blur tool.

• Use the left or right bracket keys on your keyboard to get a small-sized brush.

• In the Options bar, set the "Strength" to 100%.

• Brush along the edges of the subject to soften those edges.

• If some unwanted artifacts become visible on the top layer when you make the blurred Background layer visible, select the top layer in the Layers panel, then use the Eraser tool to erase the artifacts.

Remove something from a photo

The success of this technique varies with the complexity of the shot, especially the background, and whether the subject is isolated or not. In this example, the subject is isolated, making the task easier.

1 Open an image that has something you want to remove.

2 Select the Lasso tool. In the Options bar, set "Feather" to 4 pixels. Draw a path around the subject you want removed, as shown below.

3 From the Edit menu, choose "Fill…."
Make sure "Content-Aware" is selected in the "Use" menu, then click OK. The Fill command replaces the subject with background that matches the rest of the image.

4 From the Select menu, choose "Deselect" to delete the selection.

If a seam is visible on the edge of the fill area, use the Spot Healing Brush tool to fix it, as explained on page 15. See pages 55–57 for another technique for removing something from a photo and page 58 for using the Clone Stamp tool, if appropriate for the photo.

Lose some weight

To lose weight, you need to commit to at least two or three minutes of an easy workout. Here are several quick ways to melt those pounds away without giving up whatever's in the pot. The camera adds at least ten pounds to us, so actually all we're doing is making ourselves look like we do in person.

Use a simple Transform operation

1   Open an image file. Press Command A (PC: Control A) to select all of the image.

2   From the Edit menu, choose "Free Transform." This makes the transform bounding box appear with control handles on the edges.

3   Drag each of the side control handles in toward the center of the image just a bit (see below).

4   When you are satisfied with the image, hit the Enter key. Press Command D (PC: Control D) to make the bounding box disappear.

Transform distorts the image slightly, but would you notice?

***To crop** the excess white space from the sides of the image, select the image with the Rectangular Marquee tool, then go to the Image menu and choose "Crop."*

—continued

Or use Content-Aware Scale

There are several techniques using Content-Aware scaling in this chapter. This is an alternative to the technique on the previous page.

1   Open an image file.

2   From the Select menu, choose "All."

3   From the Edit menu, choose "Content-Aware Scale." This puts a bounding box around the image with handles on the corners and sides.

4   Drag the side control handles in toward the center of the image.

    When you like the result, hit the Enter key to commit it.

5   You'll probably want to crop the image when you're done: select the image with the Rectangular Marquee tool, then go to the Image menu and choose "Crop" (also see pages 82–85).

Content-Aware Scaling distorts the entire image, but a little differently from Free Transform (on the previous page).

Or use the Liquify filter

1 Open an image file.

2 From the Filter menu, choose "Liquify…." The image opens in the "Liquify" window, shown below.

 3 Select the *Forward Warp* tool (the top tool in the toolbox). Set the brush *Size, Density,* and *Pressure* on the right. Experiment.

4 The brush outline appears in the preview window. Drag the brush toward an edge of an object you want to move. To make an object thinner, such as an arm, gently work both sides of the arm, pushing pixels toward each other.

5 To protect an area from being distorted, such as the bowl in this image, first paint it with the *Freeze Mask* tool (see the callout below). When you drag the Liquify brush near a red "frozen" area, the pixels under the red mask are protected, as shown below.

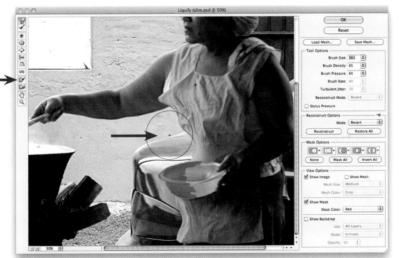

This exaggerated brush stroke shows the Liquify effect.

Here is the final result of five minutes with the Liquify filter. Learn more about Liquify on page 202.

Liquify text

The Liquify filter shown on the previous page is not just for images. Try it on text. (There is lots more about text in Chapter 6.)

1 Open a new, blank document.

 2 Select the Type tool in the Tools panel. Click on the bottom-left side of the document; this sets a flashing insertion point for typing and also creates a new text layer in the Layers panel.

3 From the Window menu, choose "Character" to open the Character panel (shown below).

Choose a font and font size, then type some text in the document window.

4 Make sure the text layer is selected in the Layers panel. Then from the Filter menu, choose "Liquify…." You will be asked to rasterize the text; click OK.

Experiment with the tools and settings to brush or click on the text, shown below. Click OK when you're finished.

Choose tools here.

Modify brush settings here.

Create unique images with the Filter Gallery

The Filter Gallery contains a large collection of filters, and each filter has adjustable settings that multiply the number of effects you can apply by hundreds. Or maybe millions (we're not finished counting).

1 Open an image.

2 From the Filter menu, choose "Filter Gallery…." This opens the image in the "Filter Gallery" window, shown below.

3 Click any of the right-pointing triangles in the middle section to display the filters for that category, as shown below. Choose a filter, then experiment with the adjustments on the right.

4 **To apply multiple filters,** click the *new effect layer* icon in the bottom-right corner.

   To hide or show the effects, click the eyeball in the *Effect Layer* list (bottom-right corner).

   To change the existing effects slightly, drag the layers up or down to reorder them in the list.

5 When you're satisfied with the effect, click OK.

Filter thumbnails pane.   *Hide/show filter thumbnails pane.*

Adjustments pane.

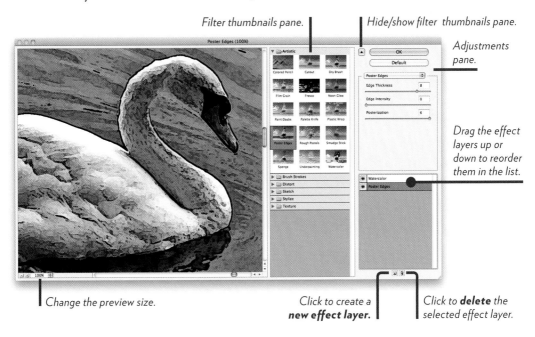

Drag the effect layers up or down to reorder them in the list.

Change the preview size.   *Click to create a* **new effect layer.**   *Click to **delete** the selected effect layer.*

43

Place an image inside text

Putting an image inside of text is a popular design technique. It requires creating a clipping mask, which may sound scary, but it's so easy to do.

1 Create a text layer: Select the Text tool and click in the document window; click on the lower left side so you have room to set the type.

2 Use the Character panel (as shown on page 42) to choose the font and size. Type some large text, as below. After you type the text, choose the Rectangular Marquee tool so you don't accidentally make more text layers every time you click.

Every time you click with the Text tool, Photoshop creates a new layer, a text layer.

3 Open an image that you want to place inside the text. The two windows will probably appear as two tabs in the same window. To separate them, drag one of the tabs off to the side until it pulls away so you have the two files, type and image, next to each other.

4 Single-click in the image file window to select it. Select the image layer in the Layers panel—single-click on it. Drag its thumbnail layer from its Layers panel over to the text file and drop it in the window. (You can now close the image file.)

5 In the file with the text, make sure the image layer is above the text layer in the Layers panel, as shown below. If not, drag the image layer above the text layer so it appears as shown below.

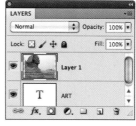

Just drag a layer up or down to move its position.

6   From the Layer menu, choose "Create Clipping Mask."

Or hover the cursor *between* the two layers, then Option-click (PC: Alt-click). The top layer becomes a clipping path that clips the image visibility *except in the text area* from the layer beneath.

The image layer thumbnail is now **indented**, a visual clue that a mask has been created. The **bent arrow** points down to the layer that is being used to clip the image. The name of the text layer is now **underlined**, indicating that it is part of the masked layer above.

7   **To reposition the image inside the text**, select the Move tool from the Tools panel (it's the tool at the very top). Make sure the image layer is selected, then drag the image to reposition it within the text.

The text is actually still editable. See Chapter 6 for details on working with text.

8   **To create a dramatic black background** for the type, create a new layer: From the Layer menu, choose New > Layer…. Click OK.

Drag that layer to the bottom of the Layers panel, as shown below.

Fill that layer with black: First, select the layer. Then, to make sure the *Foreground* color is black, tap the D key. From the Edit menu, choose Fill > Foreground Color. Ta da!

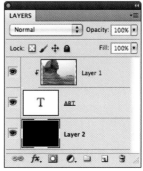

Add Layer Styles for special effects

When you attach a **Layer Style** to a layer, it affects everything on that layer. A layer style can be a drop shadow, bevel and emboss, a glow, or any other effect. You can create a text layer and add a style to it, or create a shape into which you will insert something later, an object on a transparent layer (see Chapter 9 about transparency), or even a graphic from Illustrator or an EPS file. In this example, we're using a small Illustrator drawing. See more about Layer Styles on pages 102–105.

1   The document shown below has a sunset image as a background layer. I created the Cupid layer by dragging the Cupid graphic straight from an open Adobe Illustrator document into this Photoshop window of the sunset. You can also use the "Place…" command in the File menu to place something like an Illustrator file or an EPS.

   If the file appears with an X through it, you must hit the Enter key before you can do anything else.

2   To add one or more *Layer Styles,* double-click the layer to which you want the styles to apply. The Layer Style dialog opens.

   Select a style from the Styles pane: Click its checkbox, and *then single-click its name* so you can set the controls for that style in the center pane. Click OK when done.

We've added four different styles to the Cupid layer.

46

3   As you can see in the image and in the Layers panel, below, we added a drop shadow, an inner glow, bevel and emboss, and a color stroke.

To move the image, *make sure its layer is selected. Then tap the V key and drag the image.*

When a layer has a layer style attached, an *fx* icon appears on the right side of the layer.

To copy a layer style to another layer, hold down the Option key (PC: Alt key) and drag the *fx* icon from the layer it's on and drop it on the other layer.

To turn all styles off on a layer, click the eyeball icon next to "Effects."

To turn off just certain styles, click the eyeball icon next to a specific style name.

To hide/show the list of layer styles, click the small, black disclosure triangle on the right side of the layer.

TIP: Here is the easiest way to *position a drop shadow.* While the Layer Style dialog is open and the *Drop Shadow* style is selected in the Styles list, move your cursor to the image window and drag the shadow to the position you want, right on the image.

Replace the picture on a wall

Eventually you'll want to replace a painting on a gallery wall to show how your work would look in that space. Or you'll want to replace the framed photo of your ex that's in the background of your children's photo. There's more than one way to do it, but this way is quick, easy, and straightforward.

1 Open an image to modify.

2 Find the file you want to use as a replacement. You can drag it from your Desktop right into the document window, *or* open a second file, separate the two tabs, and drag the image layer from one file into the other. The new element is automatically placed on a new layer.

Drag an image file icon from your computer into a Photoshop window to create a new layer containing that image file.

3 Select the new layer, if it isn't already. **To make it easier to see the shapes,** set the layer Opacity to 50% or lower.

From the Edit menu, choose Transform > Distort (this particular transformation enables you to drag the corners individually and distort the image as necessary).

Drag each corner handle and match the corners up with the corners of the existing image.

Drag the corners to distort the image.

4 When the new image looks the same size and shape as the original, hit Enter to commit the transformation.

Change the layer Opacity back to 100%.

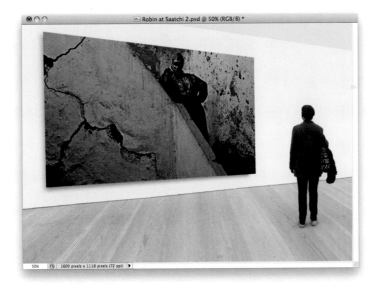

Note: After you commit the transformation, the layer thumbnail displays a small icon in its bottom-right corner to indicate the layer is a *Smart Object*. That's not important in this example, but a very useful thing for many projects. Learn about Smart Objects on pages III–II3.

Colorize a photo

You'll often want to adjust the color of an image, either for color accuracy or for effect. Here are some simple and easy techniques for several different types of colorization. (Also see page 66 for hand-tinting a photograph.)

Open an image that you want to experiment on by colorizing. It can be anything from vegetables to old family photos to the moon. Then follow the steps for one of the three techniques on the following pages.

Modify color using a Hue/Saturation Adjustment Layer

1 Select the layer you want to colorize (if you just opened a new file, it is probably the *Background* layer).

2 At the bottom of the Layers panel, click the *new Adjustment Layer* icon (shown left and below), then choose "Hue/Saturation..." from the menu that pops up. *Or* from the Layer menu, choose New Adjustment Layer > Hue/Saturation.

3 A new Adjustment Layer appears in the
   Layers panel and the Adjustments panel
   opens. The color range menu, circled to
   the right, is set by default to "Master"
   (all colors).

   Drag the *Hue* slider left or right to change
   the overall color palette of the image.

   Drag the *Saturation* slider to the left to
   *de*saturate all colors (all the way to the
   left removes all color) and to the right
   to saturate the colors more.

4 **To make changes to specific color ranges,**
   change the "Master" color range to one
   of the other colors in the pop-up menu, such as *Greens.* Now when
   you drag a slider, it affects that specific color range.

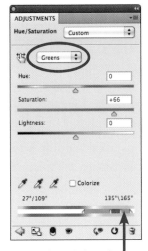

ADVANCED TIP: Experiment with the color
spectrum graph at the bottom of the panel.
The spectrum sliders show the color range
selected.

For instance, choose a color from the
"Master" menu (circled, left).

Drag the sliders in the *middle* of the
spectrum to expand or contract the
color range.

Drag the *outside* sliders to increase
or decrease the amount of *falloff* (how
gradually the changes affect nearby colors).

You can judge the effect by watching the
live preview in the image window.

*Get very specific with the color
changes using the spectrum sliders.*

Paint with the Color Replacement tool

This is another way to colorize a photo. As on page 50, open an image you want to experiment on. In this example, we're going to turn some of the zucchini gold.

1 In our example, we want to first exaggerate the highlights so the light gold color will show effectively and dramatically. If you want to do this to your own photo, follow along with us:

Select the Dodge tool in the Tools panel, shown on the left—this tool lightens areas as you brush with it.

In the Options bar, set the "Range" pop-up menu to *Highlights,* then set the "Exposure" setting to around *15%.*

From the Brush Preset picker in the Options bar, assign the Dodge tool a very soft edge: Drag the *Hardness* slider all the way to the left, to zero.

Brush gently in the highlight areas of your image. Now you're ready to colorize. (Of course, you could skip all of that if you don't need more highlight areas.)

2 Set the Foreground color to the color of your choice: Single-click the *Foreground* color swatch in the Tools panel (in the illustration on the left, it's yellow; yours might be black or some other color).

Select the color from the color picker that opens. We chose a yellow gold for the zucchini. Click ok.

3 Select the Color Replacement tool in the Tools panel. It resides under the regular Brush tool, so either *press* on the Brush tool or right-click on it to reveal the other brushes in a pop-out menu.

4 In the Options bar, settings for color replacement appear. Set the "Mode" pop-up menu to *Color,* set the "Limits" pop-up menu to *Find Edges,* and set the "Tolerance" to *30%.* The Tolerance setting determines to what degree similar-colored pixels will be replaced.

5 The three eyedropper tools in the Options bar determine how pixel colors are *sampled,* or read, for color replacement, as explained on the next page.

Sampling options.

The **first** eyedropper icon selects **continuous sampling**: As you drag the Color Replacement tool across the image, it continuously resamples pixels underneath the brush and replaces them with the *Foreground* color. (Enlarge or reduce the size of your brush by tapping the [or] keys.)

The **second** eyedropper icon samples **once per click**: Whatever color is under the tool when you single-click on the image is the only color that gets replaced with the Foreground color (the Tolerance setting affects how many similar colors also get replaced).

The **third** eyedropper icon replaces only areas that contain the *Background* box color. If you want to use this option, which is pretty amazing, first select the Eyedropper tool from the Tools panel and Option-click* on a color in your image that you want to use as the *background* color, which will be replaced; you should see the *Background* swatch color change. Now single-click* on the *Foreground* swatch and choose a color; click ok (*or* single-click the Eyedropper on a color in the image). Now you're ready to choose the Color Replacement brush and paint with it. Experiment with changing, say, the color of a shadow using this option.

6 To continue this experiment, select the first Sampling option, *Continuous.* Start brushing in the areas where you want to replace color. As long as the crosshair in the middle of the Color Replacement tool doesn't cross over into the background (where it will immediately sample a new color and replace it), the tool will do a good job of detecting edges and stopping there.

＊TIP: If the Option-click chooses a Foreground color instead of a Background color, it's because in your Colors panel the Background swatch is selected (see pages 188–189) and that messes up this keyboard shortcut. Tap the D key to select the Foreground color box in both the Tools panel and the Color panel at the same time, then try the technique again.

Use "Colorize" in the Hue/Saturation Adjustment panel

Here is yet another way to colorize a photo. In this example, we're going to make the zucchini looks as if it is printed with an expensive but fake (and very quick) duotone effect. A duotone is a print made with (usually) a black-and-white photo with another color layered into it, creating very rich images. There are more complicated ways to make gorgeous duotones in Photoshop, but here is a quick and simple version.

As on the previous pages, open an image you want to experiment on.

1 Select the layer you want to colorize (if you just opened a new file, it is probably the *Background* layer).

2 At the bottom of the Layers panel, click the *New Adjustment Layer* icon (shown to the left), then choose "Hue/Saturation…" from the menu that pops up. *Or* from the Layer menu, choose New Adjustment Layer > Hue/Saturation.

3 In the Adjustments panel that opens, check the *Colorize* box.

4 Drag the *Hue* and *Saturation* sliders until you're satisfied with the results.

Colorize simulates a duotone effect in any color you choose.

Remove a subject from a photo

The difficulty of this varies with the complexity of the shot, especially the background, and whether the subject is isolated or not. When the background is a smooth gradation or a solid color, the task is easier. (Also see pages 38 and 58 for other techniques to do something similar.)

1   Open an image from which you want to remove someone.

2   Single-click the *Quick Mask Mode* icon at the bottom of the Tools panel (shown to the left).

3   Select the Brush tool. Use the Brush Preset picker in the Options bar to choose a brush *Size;* set the *Hardness* to 100% so it has a hard edge.

In the Options bar, set the *Opacity* and the *Flow* both to 100%.

4   Paint the subjects you plan to *keep* in the photo. Remember, you can tap the right and left bracket keys to change the brush size. The red color is the default mask color.

To paint strands of hair, enlarge the image (Command +) (PC: Control +) and use a very small brush size (a pressure-sensitive tablet makes a world of difference when doing this sort of thing).

TIP: Occasionally it's helpful to temporarily **rotate the canvas** as you paint. To do so, tap the R key to activate the Rotate tool; drag on the image with the Rotate tool. Switch back to the Brush tool (B) to continue painting.

To straighten the image, tap R, then drag to straighten it. Hold down the Shift key to force the image to snap to 90° increments. Tap B to get the brush back.

— continued

5 Click the *Quick Mask Mode* icon again to turn off the red color and convert the selection to a marching-ants border.

Everything in the image *except* the masked area is selected, but we need just the opposite. So from the Select menu, choose "Inverse" to invert the selection. Now our subjects are selected.

6 In the Layers panel, make sure the image layer is selected. Then from the Layer menu, choose New > Layer via Copy. A new layer is created that contains the subjects on a transparent background.

7 Create another new layer: In the Layers panel, single-click the *New layer* icon at the bottom of the panel (circled, above).

Drag this new, empty layer *below* the transparent layer of your subject/s.

8   We plan to fill this layer with a gradient that will simulate the
    original background, so we first need to select a *Foreground* and
    a *Background* color, as follows.

    Set the *Foreground* color: Choose the Eyedropper tool and click
    on the left side of the background in the image.

    Set the *Background* color: Option-click (PC: Alt-click) the other side
    of the background image.

    Your Foreground/Background swatches at the almost-bottom of the
    Tools panel should be displaying your colors.

9   Select the Gradient tool in the Tools panel.

    In the Options bar, single-click the *Gradient picker* (shown below).
    From the dialog box that appears, select the "Foreground to
    Background" swatch from the pop-up menu (it's the one in the
    upper-left corner of the Presets). Click OK.

    In the Options bar, single-click the *Linear Gradient* option, shown
    below.

Gradient picker.   Linear Gradient.

10 Position the Gradient tool in the new, empty layer and drag horizon-
    tally from far left to far right, across the background. The layer is
    filled with the gradient, magically behind your subject/s. Wow.

11 To add a bit of realism, try adding some film grain or noise to the
    background blend:

    From the Filter menu, choose Artistic > Film Grain,
    or choose Noise > Add Noise and play with the options.

Clone something out of a photo

 The Clone Stamp is a brush that paints with an image instead of paint. You *sample* (load the tool with) something from one area of a photo and paint it into another, as shown below. The Clone Stamp is hugely useful to clean up scratches, acne, wrinkles, litter, phone lines, or even to remove unwanted people from your image (or add someone from another photo; see pages 179–181 for more details about this tool and how to use it).

1 Open an image, then create a new, blank layer to work on: From the Layer menu, choose New > Layer…. *Or* click the *Create a new layer* icon at the bottom of the Layers panel.

2 Select the Clone Stamp tool in the Tools panel.

3 In the Options bar, click the Brush Preset picker to set a brush size and hardness (choose a brush toward the soft end). Set the opacity to 100%. Click "Aligned Sample" to paint in relation to the source.

Brush preset picker.

4 Set a *clone source,* which is an area that you want to load into the Clone Stamp and repeat somewhere else: Option-click (PC: Alt-click) on a spot in the image.

5 Move the Clone Stamp to the area of the image where you want to paint a clone (a clone of grass in this example), then drag the brush on the object you want to remove/replace.

Clone source —

I Option-clicked on a spot of grass above the bottle to set the clone source.

With the clone source set, I painted over the bottle with the Clone Stamp.

For something like this, I created a new layer and cloned a sheep onto that layer. I cloned another sheep on another layer, resized that layer, and positioned the animal to appear in the distance.

Correct the dreaded red eye

Flash photography often produces an effect known as red eye. Getting rid of the red-eye effect is easy.

1   Open an image in which you want to remove the subject's red eye color (even if, as below, it wasn't caused by a camera flash).

2   Select the Red Eye tool from the Tools panel. It's hidden under the Spot Healing Brush tool (shown to the right).

3   Click in the red area of the eye. If some of the eye is still red after you click, click again in the remaining red area. Some extreme cases of red eye, such as the one below, may require three or four clicks to remove all of the red.

Click in the red part of the eye with the Red Eye tool.

Any lingering doubts that the Red Eye tool can fix your red eye photos?

The Red Eye tool is also available in the Camera Raw panel, but behaves a little differently. In Camera Raw you have a couple of adjustment sliders you can adjust, and you have to drag a rectangle around the subject's eye area. See Chapter 13 for information about Camera Raw.

Make a sky more dramatic

There are many ways to enhance the sky in a photo to make it look as vivid you remember seeing it. Some techniques are more complex than others, but also provide more control. In this chapter we want to keep it quick and simple.

1   Open an image with an average-looking sky.

2   Create a copy of the Background layer: From the Layer menu, choose New > Layer via Copy.

Or drag the Background layer and drop it on top of the *New layer* icon (circled, below). Working on a duplicate layer like this ensures that you can always get back to the original version. Turn off the visibility of the Background layer—just click its eyeball icon.

3 Choose the Quick Selection tool in the Tools panel. This tool detects edges and selects up to them. With that tool, drag in the sky area to make an automatic selection. If the entire sky is not selected, drag in the unselected area to add it to the selection.

If you need to *de*select something, hold down the Option key (PC: Alt key) and drag over the unwanted part of the selection. Use the right and left bracket keys to change your brush size as necessary.

4 From the Image menu, choose Adjustments > Shadows/Highlights…. (If you only see two sliders in this panel, check the box to "Show More Options.")

Set the "Highlights" *Amount* slider to 75% (or whatever looks best for your particular image).

To get rid of the glow that might appear around the selection edge, drag the "Highlights" *Radius* slider to 0 pixels. Click OK.

Create a panorama with Photomerge

The Photomerge™ option combines multiple photos into one panorama image (you can also merge photos vertically if you so choose). Photoshop analyzes the images and determines how best to align, merge, and blend the images together.

1 From the File menu, choose Automate > Photomerge.

2 In the Photomerge panel that opens (right), set the "Use" pop-up menu to *Files* or *Folders,* then click "Browse" to locate the files (or folder of files) to merge.

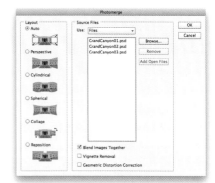

- To remove a file from the list, select it, then click "Remove."

- If the files you want are already open, click "Add Open Files."

- Select "Blend Images Together" for automatic blending of colors.

3 From the "Layout" column on the left, select a layout. The "Auto" option usually works best. Try another option if necessary.

4 Click OK.

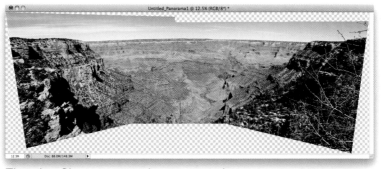

This is how Photomerge put the image together.

Cropped and brightened a bit, some cloning in the corners, and ready for framing.

Quickly juice up the color in spots

Some Photoshop users are squeamish about altering color in photos, afraid that enhancing the color or contrast is "cheating." Actually, every photo usually needs some enhancement to make it even come close to the real-world fidelity our eyes are capable of seeing. Most digital photos are far from perfect, so don't be reluctant to juice them up a bit.

When you want to quickly and easily enhance an image by saturating color in specific areas, use the Saturation tool and paint more saturation (or less) into the image.

1 Open an image in Photoshop.

2 From the Tools panel, select the Sponge tool.

3 In the Options bar (below), choose the following settings:

   • Click the Brush Preset picker to choose a brush size and hardness.

   • Set the "Mode" pop-up menu to "Saturate."

   • Click the "Flow" button to set a rate of saturation change. 100% adds a maximum amount of color saturation, lower percentages saturate colors less.

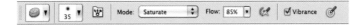

4 Use the Sponge tool to paint areas where you want the color to be stronger. If you have the Flow set too strong, or if you paint over the same area too many times, the effect can look unrealistic.

   To *desaturate* areas of the image, set the "Mode" pop-up menu to *Desaturate,* and set the "Flow" amount to a rate at which you want to apply desaturation.

Original image.

Items in the front of the basket are saturated; items in the back are desaturated.

Colorize line art

Use Layers and Layer Blending Modes to colorize the background of line art or to colorize the line art itself.

1 Open an image of line art, such as a woodcut or line drawing.

2 From the Image menu, choose Mode > RGB (or you could use CMYK, but not Grayscale).

3 Create a new layer: From the Layer menu, choose New > Layer…." Click OK.

4 Change the Blending Mode of the new layer to "Multiply" (below).

5 Click the Foreground color box in the Tools panel to select a color. Click OK.

6 Fill the new layer with the color: Make sure the new layer is selected, then from the Edit menu, choose "Fill…."

In the Fill dialog that opens, set the "Use" pop-up menu to "Foreground Color."

7 If appropriate, select the Eraser tool and erase parts of the fill color on the new layer, as shown below. Because the fill is on a different layer from the line art, you don't have to be really careful about erasing between the lines.

Blending Mode.
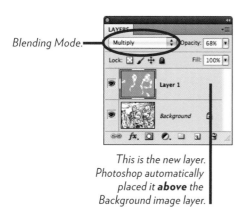

*This is the new layer. Photoshop automatically placed it **above** the Background image layer.*

To change all the dark lines to the fill color, follow the steps above but use the Blending Mode called "Screen" instead of "Multiply."

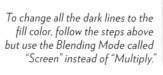

Colorize the lines instead of the background

You might want to colorize the lines in a piece of line art, instead of filling in the background. It's easy to do.

1   Open an image of line art, such as a woodcut or line drawing.

2   Create a new layer to paint on (either from the Layer menu, as in Step 3 on the opposite page, or click the *Create a new layer* icon at the bottom of the Layers panel).

3   Select that layer and change its Blending Mode to "Screen."

4   Choose the Brush tool from the Tools panel.

Use the Brush Preset picker to choose a size and hardness.

Click the Foreground color box in the Tools panel to select a color. Click OK.

5   Paint over the lines that you want in that color.

Create a new layer for each color you paint (change each layer's Blending Mode to "Screen"). This makes it easier to correct mistakes with the Eraser tool or to change colors later.

6   **To change a layer color after you've painted it,** click the *Lock Transparent pixels* button above the layers (shown below).

Select a new color in the Foreground color box.

Press Option Delete (PC: Alt Backspace). This automatically colors all pixels that are not transparent (and locked) with the new Foreground color.

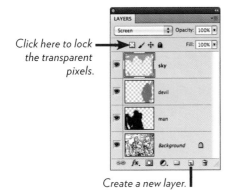

Click here to lock
the transparent
pixels.

Create a new layer.

65

Hand-tint a photo

Hand-tinted photos have an appealing quality, especially when the technique is applied to vintage photos. The example shown here starts with a scan of an old sepia-colored print. You can work on top of the original color or first convert the image to grayscale (from the Image menu, choose Adjustments > Desaturate).

1 Open an image to hand tint.

2 Create a new blank layer: From the Layer menu, choose New > Layer.

3 Change the layer Blending Mode to *Multiply.*

   NOTE: After painting (Step 5), you may decide to experiment and change the Blending Mode to something else, such as *Soft Light, Overlay,* or *Hue.* Depending on the color you use and the part of the image it's on, some Blending Modes work better than others.

4 Set the new layer's opacity to a low percentage for now, such as 30%.

5 Select the Brush tool.

   Set the Brush opacity to 100%

   Choose a Foreground color.

   Paint on the new layer, on top of an element in the image. The 30% percent layer opacity setting allows you to see through the paint color to the image below as you paint. You can adjust the layer opacity until you achieve the look you want. Remember, hand-tinted photos usually have very subtle coloring. Even though the Brush has an opacity of 100%, you can use a very low opacity percentage to create a subtle color effect.

6 Repeat Steps 2–5 for each hand-tinted color you use. By painting each color on its own layer, it's easier to adjust blending modes and opacity settings for each color.

Each color is on its own layer.

66

3 Basic Technical Stuff

WTRGB! "What The Red Green Blue" is this chapter talking about? We know you're anxious to get to the fun stuff, so we've condensed our technical Photoshop information into a painless four pages. Take a few minutes to read about the geeky stuff and you'll have a better understanding of everything you do in Photoshop.

Without getting too technical, this short chapter provides information that's helpful to know about raster and vector images, color modes (CMYK vs. RGB), image bit depth (8, 16, or 32-bit images), and image resolution (72 pixels per inch, for example).

Resolution: 300 pixels per inch.
Preferred for print projects.

Resolution: 72 pixels per inch.
This actually looks perfect when viewed on a screen.

Bitmap images

Bitmap images, also referred to as raster images, are made of a specific number of pixels in a grid. All photographs are raster images. When you use many of Photoshop's painting tools, such as a brush, airbrush, blur tool, etc., you're creating pixels in a grid. Due to the inflexible nature of a fixed grid of pixels, bitmapped images lose quality if enlarged beyond the original size—if your image prints as bitmappy or pixelated, that means the resolution is too low for the size of the graphic. The image resolution of your file, such as 72 pixels per inch for web graphics, or 300 pixels per inch for high-quality color printing, affects not only how large the file is, but also the image quality at different sizes.

If your Photoshop project is going to be viewed only on a screen, such as on a web site, photos attached to email, a digital presentation, etc., a low resolution of 72 ppi (pixels per inch) is adequate, as well as easier to edit since low-resolution images require less processing power than high-res images.

However, one issue you will discover when working in low resolution is that filter effects act differently on low-res and high-res images. A filter that looks great on a high-res image can look clunky and heavy-handed on the same image in a low-res version.

For most projects, it's better to work at actual size, in a resolution that's appropriate for the image's final destination (printed or onscreen).

Vector graphics

Vector graphics are shapes that exist as mathematical descriptions, even though they look like ordinary images on the screen. Some of Photoshop's drawing tools create vector objects. Since vector objects are mathematical descriptions, they can be enlarged to any size without any degradation of quality. When you open an Illustrator file and place it in Photoshop, it's brought in as a vector file. Text also is a vector file that can be resized up and down many times without affecting its quality. You'll notice that some operations in Photoshop will present you with a message saying that the command you requested requires *rasterizing* the object or layer—this means Photoshop must convert the mathematical description into pixels in a grid.

Color modes and file formats

RGB (red, green, blue) is the **color mode** used for images viewed on a screen, such as on web pages and presentations. Many home and office printers also print files that use the RGB color space. Some Photoshop filters work only in RGB mode.

CMYK (cyan, magenta, yellow, black) is the **color mode** for documents printed on expensive color laser printers or in full color by commercial printers.

- **To set the color mode for a document,** go to the Image menu, choose "Mode," then select *RGB Color* or *CMYK Color.* Other common choices are "Grayscale" for images that don't require color, and "Indexed Color" for web files such as GIF images.

Some RGB colors cannot be duplicated by printing presses. An image with wild RGB colors will undergo a drastic color shift when you convert the file to CMYK. If you plan to send an image to press, avoid shocking surprises: To have Photoshop **simulate CMYK colors, even as you work in RGB mode,** go to the View menu and choose Proof Setup > Working CMYK.

Save your document in the proper **file format** for its intended use:

- Save in the **TIFF file format** for professional printing.
- Save as **JPEG** or **JPG file format** for any document that will be viewed on a monitor or video screen of any sort.
- Save as the **native file format, PSD,** to retain all layer and image editing capabilities so you can work on it again.

Bit depth

Bit depth is how much color information can potentially be stored in each pixel of an image. Higher bit depth values mean more color information and more accurate color. An 8-bpc (bits per channel) RGB file is called a 24-bit file because RGB files have three color channels, and if each channel is 8-bpc, that equals 24 bits of color information data for each pixel.

Photoshop can work with 8, 16, and 32-bpc images. A 32-bpc image is referred to as High Dynamic Range (HDR). Unless you're a professional photographer, you probably are working mostly with 8-bpc images.

Many, but not all, Photoshop features and filters work on 16-bpc images. If you encounter a situation in which you need to apply a problematical filter to a 16-bit image, convert the file to an 8-bpc (go to Image > Mode > 8 Bits/Channel), apply the filter, then save as a copy, to preserve the original 16-bpc file.

Image resolution

To set the image resolution, from the Image menu, choose "Image Size...." In the "Image Size" dialog that opens (below, left), enter a value in the "Resolution" field. **For high quality printing**, set the resolution to 300 ppi (pixels per inch); **for onscreen images**, set it to 72 ppi (see the example in the bottom area of the page).

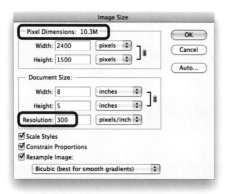 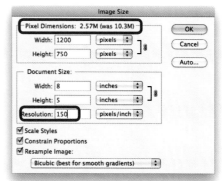

If the resolution is cut in half, to 150 pixels, the "Width" and "Height" pixel values shown at the top of the dialog are also cut by half (above right). But the "Document Size" dimensions are still the same, 8 inches by 5 inches. This means that the document stays the same measurable size, but there are half as many pixels to render the image.

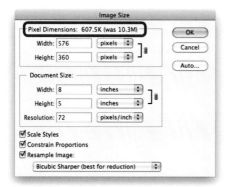

The image file size (circled) gets smaller as the *Resolution* value gets smaller. This file, originally 10.3 megabytes, is now 607.5 kilobytes.

To size this image for the web, set the resolution to 72 ppi (as shown above). The pixel dimensions of the image are now very small, compared to the 300 ppi version or the 150 ppi versions at the top of the page. This low resolution works great for viewing on a computer screen. A higher resolution would mean a much larger file (*larger* as in more megabytes), without better quality on the screen.

4 Select & Transform

In Photoshop, you'll find yourself doing two things over and over again. The first is **selecting** elements to modify them. Photoshop provides many different ways to select images or parts of images, and how you select an item can determine what you can do with it. The second is **transforming** elements. The transform commands in Photoshop—scale, rotate, skew, distort, perspective, warp, and flip—enable you to modify images in almost unlimited ways.

Experiment with selecting and cropping in this chapter. Photoshop can only undo that very last thing you did, so work on a photo you don't care about. If you don't save your changes to the image, you can always "Revert" to the original image from the File menu. Or, to preserve the original, you can also make a copy of the file you want to work on (and in Chapter 7 you'll learn how the History panel provides the equivalent of multiple undos).

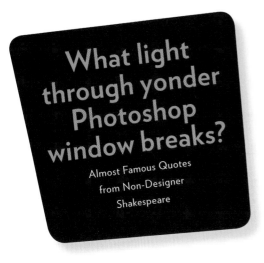

What light through yonder Photoshop window breaks?

Almost Famous Quotes from Non-Designer Shakespeare

Selection tools

Shown below are the four main selection tools (and their variants) in the Tools panel: the **Marquee** tools, the **Lasso** tools, and the **Quick Selection** tools. To display the pop-up menus of the hidden tools, *press* (don't click) or right-click on tool icons that have a small triangle in the bottom-right corner.

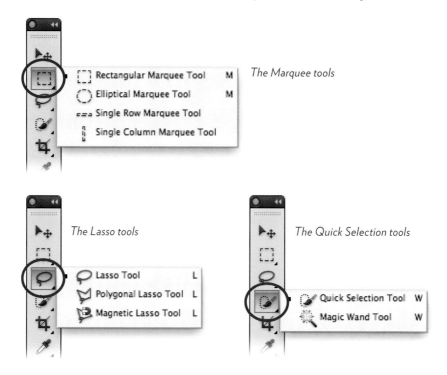

The Marquee tools

The Lasso tools

The Quick Selection tools

We include the **Crop** tool as a selection tool because it selects parts of an image, then transforms it. (The **Slice** tools hidden beneath the Crop tool are used to slice images apart for web pages, a specialized feature we don't cover in this book.)

The **Pen** tool is an important selection tool because you can use it to draw paths around elements, then convert those paths to selections that you can save and edit endlessly. See pages 80–81.

> TIP: **To deselect your entire selection** at any point, use the keyboard shortcut Command D (PC: Control D), *or* go to the Select menu and choose "Deselect."

The Rectangular Marquee tool

Select the **Rectangular Marquee** tool. Drag to draw a marquee around an area that you want to select. As with any rectangular tool, drag diagonally to create the shape.

With the selection made, you can modify just the selection in any way. For instance, you can crop the image: From the Image menu, choose "Crop."

The Elliptical Marquee tool

The **Elliptical Marquee** tool acts the same as above, except that it draws circles and ovals. As above, any modifications you make will apply to just the selected shape. For instance, you can desaturate the selection: From the Image menu, choose Adjustments > Desaturate.

TIP: **To make a selection *outward* from the *center*** of any marquee tool, hold down the Option key (PC: Alt key) as you drag.

TIP: **To constrain the shape to a perfect square or circle,** hold down the Shift key.

Single Row or Single Column Marquee tool

Click in an image with the **Single Row Marquee** or **Single Column Marquee** tool to select a row or column one-pixel wide (below-left). This is useful when you need to trim just a tiny wee bit from the edge of an image—instead of selecting the rest of the image and cropping that wee edge, use one of these tools to select just the edge. Or use it to add or subtract from an existing selection (see page 78). To create graphic design effects, fill the selection with color, add a stroke of color to the selection, or do both, as shown below.

Selection with stroke and fill applied. ➡

Selection. ➡

Selection with two strokes applied. ➡

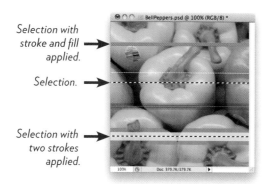

Multiple Single Row selections.

To stroke or fill a selection with color, *right-click it, then select "Fill" or "Stroke" and choose your options. (You must right-click while the selection is **active**.)*

When a marquee tool is selected, these buttons in the Options bar let you (from the left) make a new selection, add to selection, subtract from selection, and intersect with selection (see page 78).

The Lasso tool 🔍

Use the **Lasso tool** to draw freehand shapes around a selection when pinpoint accuracy is not critical. This is a useful tool for selecting elements that don't fit nicely inside a circular or rectangular selection.

1　Select the Lasso tool in the Tools panel.

2　Draw a path around a part of the image.

The Polygonal Lasso tool

The regular Lasso tool can be difficult to control with a mouse, but the **Polygonal Lasso** tool is another easy way to draw a complicated path. It only draws straight lines between clicks of the mouse.

1 Select the Polygonal Lasso tool.

2 Click once in the image.

3 Click a second time and a selection line appears between the two clicks. Every time you click, another straight line connects that point to the previous point.

4 To close the path and make the selection, click on the original first-click point. *Or* double-click—wherever you double-click, that line will snap to the beginning point.

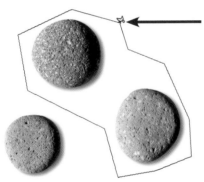

When you are close enough to the beginning point, this tiny little open dot will appear next to the lasso. That is your visual clue that you can now click and the path will close.

The Magnetic Lasso tool

The **Magnetic Lasso tool** is hidden under the Lasso tool. Select it, then trace along an edge. The path it draws snaps to the edge like a magnet. This tool is not very accurate unless the image is a very high contrast image, so experiment with it, for instance, on hard-edge brush strokes you've made or on elements in an image that show a strong contrast between its colors and the background.

Feather the edge (make it soft and fuzzy)

A soft-edged or *feathered* selection is useful for special effects and for subtly blending a foreground image into a background. Feathered edges also enable you to create a montage of different images that blend seamlessly together.

This selection has a Feather setting of 40 pixels. Edges this soft almost disappear when overlayed on another image.	When you copy and paste a feathered selection into another image (above), the two images blend together seamlessly.

To make a feathered selection, choose your selection tool, then set an amount in the "Feather" field in the Options bar. Experiment with a 5 px feather, and then with a 20 px feather. You'll notice that the selection has rounded corners, your visual clue that a feather is being used.

Add a feather after you've made a selection

If you need to feather a selection after you've drawn it, do this:

1 From the Select menu, choose Modify > Feather.

2 In the little dialog that appears, enter the amount of feathering you want to apply. There's no preview, so you have to guess how much "Feather Radius" to use.

Adjust a feather after you've made a selection

Not only can you add a feather after you've made the selection, this dialog
lets you adjust the settings and preview them before committing.

1 In the Options bar, click the "Refine Edge…" button (circled below),
   which brings up a dialog.

2 In the Refine Edge dialog (below, left), set a Feather amount.

3 Choose how you want to preview the results: Single-click the *View*
   well in the "View Mode" section of the dialog (below, right).

4 Make your adjustments and click OK.

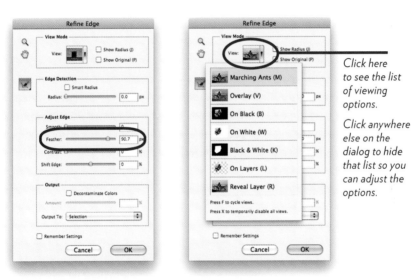

*Click here
to see the list
of viewing
options.*

*Click anywhere
else on the
dialog to hide
that list so you
can adjust the
options.*

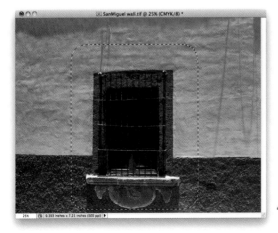

This is a "Marching
Ants" preview, where
the selection boundary
looks like ants marching
around the page.

***To see an actual
preview of the soft
edge,*** choose the
"Overlay" preview mode.

Modify your selection

In the Options bar, you have some great settings for modifying the selection. Experiment with these! They are hugely useful.

A B C D

A **New selection.** This option is chosen by default. When you drag to select, existing selections are released. To *add* to a selection, hold down the Shift key as you drag multiple selections.

To *subtract* from a selection, hold down the Option key (PC: Alt key) as you drag.

TIP: If your selection isn't acting as you think it should, check to see which button is highlighted.

B **Add to selection.** Select this icon, then drag to select something. Each dragged selection is added to existing selections. You can make two or more *separate* selections this way, or you can *overlap* an existing selection to add to it.

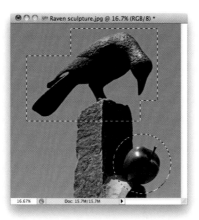

To make this selection, I first used the Rectangular Marquee tool to drag the top-right rectangular shape.

Then I dragged the lower-left overlapping rectangular shape.

Then I switched to the Elliptical Marquee tool, clicked the *Add to selection* button, then added two other shapes (the second rectangle and the circle).

C **Subtract from selection.** Select this icon, then drag a shape to *deselect* part of an existing selection.

D **Intersect the selection.** This selects only where the new selection intersects with the original selection.

TIP: **To deselect everything,** use the keyboard shortcut: Command D (PC: Control D).

The Quick Selection tool

With the **Quick Selection tool**, *brush* on the image and the tool automatically detects and selects up to the edges of the element you brush on. If the image has well-defined edges, this works great.

1 Choose the Quick Selection tool.

2 In the Brush Preset picker in the Options bar (shown below), choose a brush size and hardness (closer to zero is softer).

3 Brush inside an area to select it. **To add to the selection**, pick up the mouse and drag again in an unselected area (by default, the *Add to selection* option stays selected after the first brush stroke).

4 **To subtract from the selection**, select the *Subtract from selection* icon in the Options bar, then brush across unwanted areas.

5 If it's necessary to refine the selection, use the options in the "Refine Edge…" dialog from the Options bar (see page 77).

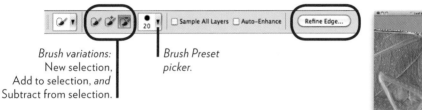

Brush variations:
New selection,
Add to selection, *and*
Subtract from selection.

Brush Preset picker.

The Magic Wand tool

The **Magic Wand tool** is very similar to the Quick Selection tool, above, except you can refine the selection before you begin. Choose the Magic Wand, then in the Options bar:

• Set the "Tolerance" level to a low number to limit the color selection close to the first color on which you click; set a higher number to grab more colors outside that original range.

• Check "Anti-alias" for a smoother edge.

• **To select all similar colors in the image** with one click, uncheck "Contiguous" (if "Contiguous" is checked, only similar colors that are touching are selected).

Just single-click to select an area; click in another area to select more.

> **TIP:** **To select all similar colors,** go to the Select menu and choose "Similar."

The Pen tool

To learn to use the Pen tool, see pages 160–163. The Pen tool is very different from any other tool. If you use a Pen tool in InDesign or Illustrator, you'll find this one similar.

 When you draw with the Pen tool, Photoshop automatically stores a *path* in the Paths panel. If you don't see the Paths panel on your screen, choose "Paths" from the Window menu.

You can have many paths on an individual Paths layer (although if they are unrelated to each other, make separate layers for each one). You can apply a fill and stroke to any path, but the fill and stroke do not stick to the path itself—they appear on another layer as raster images.

We often draw a path around irregular objects (or people) that we want to separate from a background. The path we draw can be made into a selection, then we can use that selection to delete the background. For instance, in the example below, we want to put the stones on a layer by themselves, so we can add whatever background we want. I've drawn a path around each stone. All three paths are on one *path layer* in the Paths panel.

1 Open an image, then open the Paths panel (as mentioned above).

2 Click the *Create new path* button at the bottom of the Paths panel.

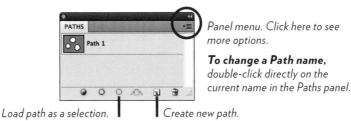

Panel menu. Click here to see more options.

To change a Path name, *double-click directly on the current name in the Paths panel.*

Load path as a selection.   Create new path.

3 With the new path layer selected, select the Pen tool in the Tools panel and draw a path around each stone.

In this example, we're going to delete the background. But with the selection made, you can copy either the selection or its inverse, apply effects and filters to the selected area, change the colors, and so on.

4   Click the *Load path as a selection* button (bottom of the Paths panel). The path turns into a marching ants selection.

5   The stones are selected, but we want to inverse the selection so we can delete the image background: From the Select menu, choose "Inverse" (below, left).

6   Press Delete to erase the image background.

   If the stones are on a *Background layer,* the background is replaced by the current Background color.

   If the stones are on a regular layer, the background is replaced by transparency (shown below, right). We can now create another layer below the stones layer, and fill it with a new background color or image.

Background selected.   *Background deleted.*

7   To add drop shadows, double-click the stones layer and select the "Drop Shadow" option in the Layer Style dialog (see pages 102–103).

Using the Pen tool and the Paths palette, I separated the image of the woman from the background. InDesign is able to wrap text around the path that I created in Photoshop. Too amazing.

An example of how to use a path in Photoshop to wrap a caption (above) in InDesign.

The Crop tool

The **Crop tool** is not a selection tool, but it is one you will use very often in combination with selecting.

You can crop an image in two quick steps without the Crop tool if all you want to do is get rid of an unnecessary part of an image:

1   With the Rectangular Marquee tool, select an area that contains the element you want to *keep* (make sure there is no feather on the selection; see page 76).

2   From the Image menu, choose "Crop." Ta da.

For more specific cropping, the **Crop tool** provides much more control. You can set the specific dimensions and resolution of the cropped area, and you can see a preview of the results.

1   Choose the Crop tool from the Tools panel.

2   In the Options bar, set the "Width" and "Height" that you want the finished image to be (or see the tip below).

    For a measurement in inches, type "in" after the number.
    For a measurement in pixels, type "px" after the number.

3   You can set the "Resolution" if you understand clearly how it might affect the image. If not, leave it blank.

    Set 300 pixels/inch if the image is to be printed in high-quality; set 72 pixels/inch for screen viewing.

Click to clear all the fields
in the Options bar.

TIP: If you leave the fields blank, Photoshop will maintain the current resolution of the image and resize according to the crop area that you draw with the tool.

4　Drag a rectangle around the area you want to crop, as shown below. If you have set a width and height, your rectangle will be limited to proportions matching that shape.

Press in the middle to **move** the crop area to another part of the image.

Resize it by dragging a corner handle; hold down the Shift key to keep the same proportion.

5　Once the crop area is drawn, the Options bar changes, as shown.

If you are on a regular layer, not a Background layer, you can choose to *Delete* or *Hide*. The *Hide* option allows you to later reposition the image within the cropped area: just move the image with the Move tool. (To convert a Background layer to a regular layer *before* you crop, double-click "Background" in the Layers panel, then click OK.)

6　Set the "Crop Guide Overlay" pop-up menu to *None, Rule of Thirds,* or *Grid*. The *Rule of Thirds,* a design theory that says compositional elements should fall within a grid of thirds, visually divides the crop area into thirds.

7　Check "Shield" if you want to shade the part of the image that will be deleted or hidden, as you can see above. Set a shield *Color* (default black works best), and set the *Opacity* of the shield to your taste.

8　**To commit** the current crop operation, hit the Enter key (or click the checkmark icon you see farther to the right in the Options bar).

To cancel, hit the Esc key (or click the Cancel icon next to the checkmark, as mentioned above).

To make the selection marquee disappear, click anywhere.

Crop based on another image

This is very useful when you have a number of photographs in a project that all need to be the same size. For instance, perhaps you have a number of staff member photos, and you want all their heads to be positioned in approximately the same area of the photo and about the same size.

1 Select the Crop tool in the Tools panel, then crop and size an image as you want.

2 Single-click the "Front Image" button in the Options bar.

3 Open another image, then drag the Crop tool, which is now constrained to the previous image's dimensions and resolution, to encompass the part of the image you want to preserve. It's up to you to position the cropping box to set someone's head, for instance, in the same position as the first image.

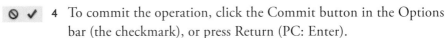 4 To commit the operation, click the Commit button in the Options bar (the checkmark), or press Return (PC: Enter).

To cancel the operation, click the Cancel icon in the Options bar (shown on the left), or hit the Escape key.

Before cropping.

After cropping.

Solomon Catt   Serena Pickering Catt   Riley Adkins Catt   Lydia Alice Beeson Catt

Crop in perspective

The "Perspective" checkbox used with the Crop tool not only allows you to crop the image, but make lens corrections at the same time. This is useful, for instance, when an image is distorted in the camera or because it was shot at an extreme angle. We often ignore lens distortion, especially when it occurs in personal photos, but occasionally you may want to fix it. If you don't adjust the lens distortion as you crop the image, you can adjust it later using one of the Transform tools, Distort or Perspective (see page 89). The Transform tools are a better choice for some images, because the Perspective Crop tool may crop away more of the image than you want (as shown below-right).

1 Open an image in which there is lens distortion.

2 Select the Crop tool.

3 Drag a rectangle around the image.

4 Check the "Perspective" box in the Options bar. ☑ Perspective

Drag the corners of the cropping area to align with the image perspective, as shown below-left.

5 To commit the crop operation, click the Commit button (the checkmark) in the Options bar, or hit Return (PC: Enter).

To cancel the operation, click the Cancel icon in the Options bar (shown on the left), or hit the Escape key.

Transform commands

As you can see in the Edit menu, there are two main Transform items, "Free Transform," which applies to a *selected layer,* and "Transform" with a submenu of options, all of which apply to *individually selected items.*

Before you can transform a layer or part of an image, you *must* make a selection with one of the selection tools. To select a layer, single-click on it in the Layers panel (details on working with layers are in Chapter 5).

Transform commands in the Edit menu.

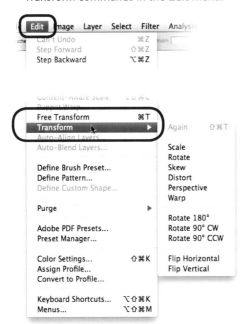

Commit or Cancel transform tasks:

- **To commit the transformation,** hit the Enter key,
  or double-click inside the bounding box,
  or click the Commit checkmark icon in the Options bar.

- **To cancel,** hit the Esc key,
  or single-click the Cancel icon in the Options bar.

- **To get rid of the selection marquee,** click anywhere,
  or press Command D (PC: Control D),
  or go to the Select menu and choose "Deselect."

Free Transform

"Free Transform" lets you do basic transforms, such as resize (scale) and rotate. Also see page 34–35 for another technique using this command.

1   Select a portion or all of the image. If you select it all, open the window wide enough that you can see the corners.

2   From the Edit menu, choose "Free Transform."

The Transform bounding box appears around the edges of the image. If you can't see the corner handles, make the window a little larger.

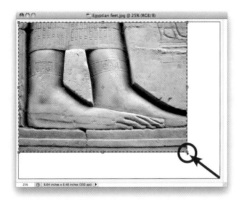

3   **To resize the selection proportionately** (to maintain its *aspect ratio*), hold down the Shift key as you drag a *corner* handle (shown above).

To resize in any way, just drag any handle. Side handles resize in just one direction; corner handles resize both sides at once.

4   **To rotate the selection,** position the cursor a few pixels away from any corner handle (you definitely have to open your window larger for this). When the cursor changes to a curved double-arrow, press-and-drag the cursor.

See page 86 for commit/ cancel options.

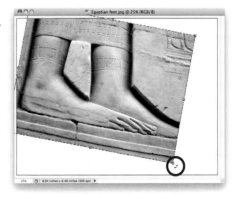

Transform menu options

From the Edit menu, choose "Transform" to access the other transform options, shown below.

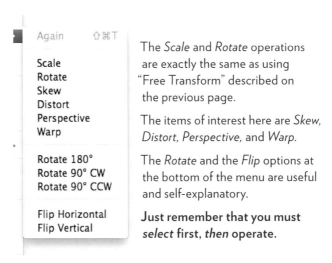

Again ⇧⌘T	The *Scale* and *Rotate* operations are exactly the same as using "Free Transform" described on the previous page.
Scale	
Rotate	
Skew	
Distort	The items of interest here are *Skew*, *Distort*, *Perspective*, and *Warp*.
Perspective	
Warp	
Rotate 180°	The *Rotate* and the *Flip* options at the bottom of the menu are useful and self-explanatory.
Rotate 90° CW	
Rotate 90° CCW	
Flip Horizontal	**Just remember that you must** *select* **first,** *then* **operate.**
Flip Vertical	

Skew a selection

Skewing an image slants it vertically or horizontally. You just never know when this might come in handy.

1   Select a portion or all of the image. If you select it all, open the window wide enough that you can see the corners.

2   From the Edit menu, choose Transform > Skew. Drag the middle handles to skew the image.

See page 86 for commit/cancel options.

Distort a selection

Distorting an image lets you drag each corner to any position, useful when you need to paste a photo into a shape in another image.

1   Select a portion or all of the image. If you select it all, open the window wide enough that you can see the corners.

2   From the Edit menu, choose Transform > Distort. Drag any corner handle to any position.

If you are matching a shape that is on another layer below this one, reduce the Opacity of this distortion layer to make it easy to align the two images. (See Chapter 5 for details about layers.)

See page 86 for commit/ cancel options.

Transform a selection in perspective

The Perspective option moves two opposite control handles equally, giving the illusion of perspective.

1   Select a portion or all of the image. If you select it all, open the window wide enough that you can see the corners.

2   From the Edit menu, choose Transform > Perspective.

3   Drag a top or bottom corner handle in toward the center; the opposite handle moves the same amount. Also experiment with dragging a corner handle downward.

See page 86 for commit/cancel options.

Warp a selection

The Warp option overlays a mesh on the image that you can manipulate. (For an advanced version, see Puppet Warp in Chapter 14.)

1 Select a portion or all of the image. If you select it all, open the window wide enough that you can see the corners.

2 From the Edit menu, choose Transform > Warp.

3 Drag any corner point or control handle to distort the mesh that overlays the image (see pages 161–163 about working with control handles).

Or drag the mesh intersections in the image interior.

Or click the "Custom" pop-up menu in the Options bar to choose from a list of preset warp options; customize the preset warp with the fields you see to the right of the "Custom" menu.

4 See page 86 for commit/cancel options.

5 All-Powerful Layers

Layers might be the most useful and powerful feature in Photoshop's extensive list of awesome features. Layers are like sheets of transparent plastic stacked on top of each other, and because layers are transparent (except where you've placed image elements or text), many layers can combine visually to create one seamless image.

You can send elements behind or in front of other elements and still change your mind later. You can hide parts of an image without harming the original, or retouch elements on a separate layer from the original, making those elements easy to delete or modify later. You can hide individual layers so they don't appear in the final piece, yet they are still in the document so you have them if necessary. You can create many versions of a single document and switch between versions effortlessly.

For example, the original Photshop file for the cover of this book puts every element on its own layer, which enables the overlapping and placement of elements such as the floating photos. Other layers in the document have their visibility turned off because they contain images that we decided not to use, including other experimental background colors.

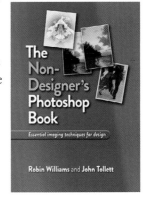

There are what Robin calls *magic layers* (Photoshop calls them *Adjustment Layers*) that actually have nothing on them that you can see, but they impact the look of the layer *beneath* without changing the pixels of the underneath layer.

While the list of layer features and techniques is longer than we can completely cover here, this chapter will give you a basic understanding of what layers can do and how to work with them.

The Layers panel

To open the Layers panel (if it isn't already), go to the Window menu and choose "Layers." *Or* click the Layers icon in the vertical Panels dock on the right side of the screen (shown below). See pages 4–6 about working with panels.

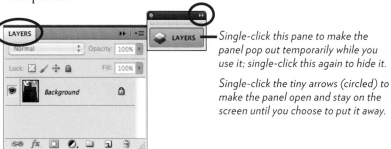

Single-click this pane to make the panel pop out temporarily while you use it; single-click this again to hide it.

Single-click the tiny arrows (circled) to make the panel open and stay on the screen until you choose to put it away.

An image might have just one layer, or it can have many layers, as shown below. It depends on how you want to work. Browse through the following layer goodies for an overview of how you might use them in your projects. When you experiment with techniques in other chapters that reference layers, come back to this chapter for the details.

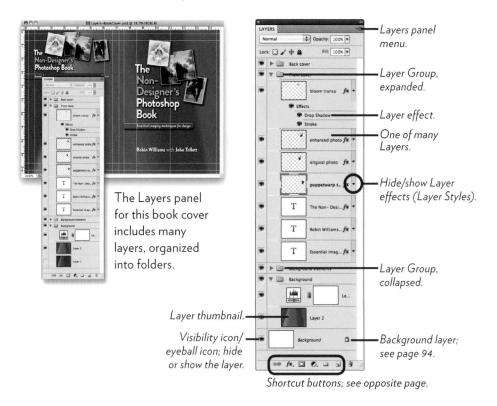

The Layers panel for this book cover includes many layers, organized into folders.

Layers panel menu.

Layer Group, expanded.

Layer effect.

One of many Layers.

Hide/show Layer effects (Layer Styles).

Layer Group, collapsed.

Background layer; see page 94.

Layer thumbnail.

Visibility icon/ eyeball icon; hide or show the layer.

Shortcut buttons; see opposite page.

The Layers panel menu

Because it's so tiny, you might not even notice the Layers panel menu, in the top-right corner of the Layers panel (circled, below-right). Click it to reveal lots of commands and options that are very useful, some of which are also represented as buttons at the bottom of the panel.

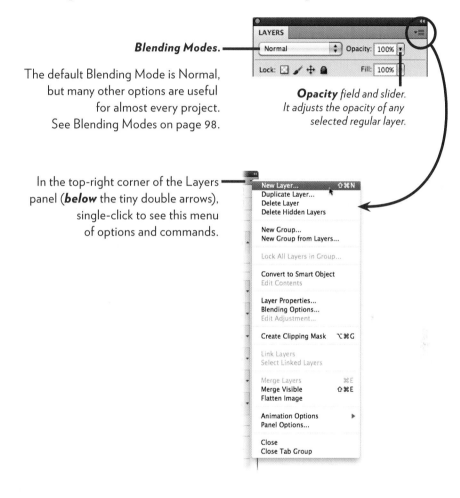

Blending Modes.

The default Blending Mode is Normal, but many other options are useful for almost every project. See Blending Modes on page 98.

Opacity field and slider. It adjusts the opacity of any selected regular layer.

In the top-right corner of the Layers panel (**below** the tiny double arrows), single-click to see this menu of options and commands.

Some of the menu options are also accessible through the buttons at the bottom of the Layers panel.

Hover over any icon to display the tool tip that describes it.

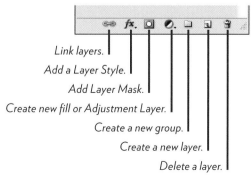

Link layers.
Add a Layer Style.
Add Layer Mask.
Create new fill or Adjustment Layer.
Create a new group.
Create a new layer.
Delete a layer.

Create and organize layers

You never run out of reasons to create another layer or two. And with all those layers stacking up, literally, you need to organize them so you can find certain layers in what can become quite a challenging mess.

The Background layer

When you create a new Photoshop document, it automatically has a layer called Background and you'll always find it at the bottom of any stack of layers you might create later.

When you open a new, blank document (as opposed to opening a photograph), the "New" dialog allows you to make the "Background Contents" either *White, Background Color,* or *Transparent.* The default is white, which obviously is not transparent, nor is any background color considered transparent. The odd thing is that a Background layer *cannot* be transparent, so if you choose *Transparent* in the New dialog, you get what's called a *regular* layer instead of one labeled "Background."

The Background layer cannot be moved from its position on the bottom, nor can you apply many of Photoshop's features. So if you try choose a command from a menu, and the command is gray (unavailable), it might be because you are trying to apply it to a Background layer.

To change the Background layer to a regular layer (a document is not required to have a Background layer) so it is more flexible, do one of the following:

- Double-click the Background layer, name it if you like (or not), and click OK.

- Drag the Lock icon on the Background layer to the Trash icon in the bottom-right corner of the Layers panel, shown below. The layer will remain, but will be renamed *Layer*.

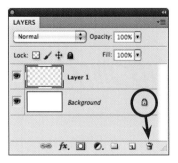

The lock icon locks either transparent pixels, image pixels, or the position of the pixels on the layer. ***Throwing away the lock icon unlocks those elements.***

To delete the whole layer, drag anywhere else in the layer and drop it in the Trash.

Create new layers

To create layers, do one of the following:

- From the Layer menu at the top of the screen, choose New > Layer…. In the dialog that opens, name the layer; click OK.

- *Or* click the *Create a new layer* icon in the bottom-right corner of the Layers panel, circled below. The new layer appears **above** the currently *selected* layer.

To create a new layer *below* the currently selected layer, Command-click (PC: Control-click) the new layer icon.

You can drag layers up or down to reorder them at any time (except the Background layer, which cannot move).

Drag-and-drop to create a new layer

Instead of using the "New Layer" dialog, you can drag and drop images into a Photoshop document.

1   Drag an image file from anywhere on your computer and drop it on a Photoshop canvas window.

    To center the new image in the canvas, hold down the Shift key as you drop it into the document window.

2   The added image appears in the window with selection crosshairs (shown below), indicating that it is a *Smart Object.* Smart Objects allow you to modify a layer without changing the original image. Learn about Smart Objects on pages 111–113.

3   Hit Enter to commit the new layer (which also makes the crosshairs disappear). A small icon appears in the layer thumbnail, indicating a Smart Object.

Drag-and-drop creates a Smart Object on a new layer.

Smart Object indicator.

Create a copy of the current layer

When you want to apply experimental features to an image, such as various filters and effects, it's often best to create a copy of that image layer and work on the copy. If a *selection* is active on the current layer, a copy of *just the selection* from that layer is placed on the new layer, making this a shortcut to isolating that element.

1 *Select* a layer or make a selection *on that layer.*

2 From the Layer menu, choose New > Layer via Copy.

Duplicate a layer

This operation is similar to creating a copy of an entire layer (not a selection) as described above, but adds a significant option. You can name the layer, but more importantly, you can save the duplicate layer in the existing document, in any document that you have open on the screen, *or* in a new document that you name here.

1 *Select* a layer in the Layers panel.

2 From the Layer menu, choose "Duplicate Layer…."

3 In the "Destination" pane, the "Document" menu lists all open documents, plus "New." Choose the document into which you want to add this layer, *or* choose "New" and name a new document.

Select the right layer

When working on an image, you often need to switch between layers. If your document contains many elements, each on its own layer, it can be difficult to quickly find the right layer to select. Here's a shortcut:

1 Choose the Move tool (V).

2 Command-click (PC: Control-click) an element in the document. This selects the layer that contains the pixels you clicked (don't *drag* with the Move tool or the image will move).

Or click the "Auto-Select" item in the Options bar (circled below). Now anywhere you click will choose the layer that contains the pixels you clicked. Don't forget to deselect this option while you're working or you'll find yourself unintentionally selecting other layers constantly.

Link layers

Placing each visual element on its own layer makes it easy to make changes to those individual pieces, but when those multiple layers combine to create one visual element, you want it to be just as easy to make changes to the *combined* visual elements (such as repositioning multiple layers at once, or changing the tranparency of multiple layers together). When you **link layers** together, in many ways they act as one layer.

In the example below, each line of handwriting is on a separate layer. To transform (move, scale, distort, or rotate) any combination of the handwritten lines as one element, first *select,* then *link* the layers.

1   Click a layer in the Layers panel to select it.
    Shift-click other layers to add them to the selection.
    This temporarily links the layers, until you select another layer.

2   To keep the layers linked, click the *Link layers* icon in the bottom-left corner of the Layers panel (circled below).

To unlink the layers, select any one of them, then click the *Link layers* icon again at the bottom of the Layers panel. Unlinking doesn't affect any changes you made while layers were linked.

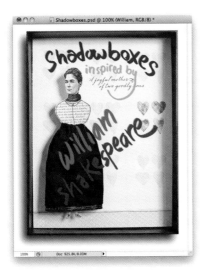

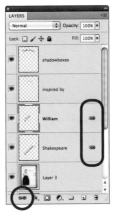

A link icon appears in each of the selected layers. Now whenever you select one of these layers, the other layer is also selected, *even if it doesn't appear highlighted.*

Use layer Blending Modes

Blending Modes affect how the pixels in one layer interact with pixels in the layers below. You can use Blending Modes in endless ways to enhance or alter images since the interaction depends on what is on the various layers, the opacity you choose for one or the other layers, the hues and colors, etc.

The file in the example below has two layers. The Background layer is a photo and the layer above it contains text. Changing the Blending Mode of the text layer alters the interaction of the text with the background image. (You cannot change the Blending Mode of the Background layer; if you want to, first make it a regular layer as explained on page 94.)

1   Open a file or create a new one in which you have at least two layers.

2   Select a layer that has a layer beneath it.

3   From the Blending Mode pop-up menu (shown below), select one of the options in the list. We chose *Vivid Light* for this example.

    To preview the effect of different Blending Modes, hold down the Shift key and tap + (the plus sign) repeatedly to toggle *down* through the list of modes. Use Shift – (minus) to cycle *up* the list.

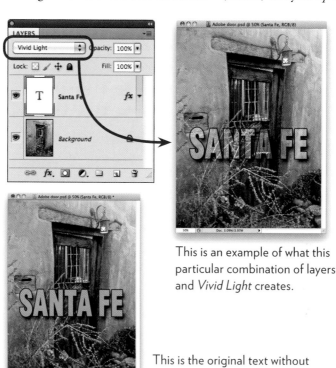

This is an example of what this particular combination of layers and *Vivid Light* creates.

This is the original text without the Blending Mode applied.

Change the visibility of layers

To toggle the visibility of layers between visible and hidden, click the eyeball icon or its well to the left of the Layer name.

When you apply preset Styles or Effects, you might see a number of new Effects listed in the Layers panel. Keep in mind you can turn individual Effects on or off for different results. Experiment!

This is a vector Shape (see page 164) with a preset Style applied. Photoshop created all the Effects you see above.

You can see where we turned off the visibility of certain effects.

Merge Visible

You can turn off the visibility of certain layers, and then combine all of the visible layers into one layer. Use the "Merge Visible" command.

1   Make sure all the layers you want to merge are *visible* (the eyeball icon appears on the left side of the layer) and the layers you do *not* want to include are *not* visible.

2   From the Layers panel menu, choose "Merge Visible."

Merge Down

You can merge two *adjacent* layers into one.

1   Make sure the layers you want to merge are *visible* (the eyeball icon appears on the left side of the layer) and that they are next to each other in the panel.

2   Select the top layer of the two.

3   From the Layers panel menu, choose "Merge Down." This will merge the *selected* layer with the layer immediately beneath.

Stamp Visible

This command is similar to "Merge Visible" explained on the previous page, but with a critical difference. It combines all visible layers into a single *new* layer, yet leaves all those original layers unchanged and still available as individual layers. You'll love this feature when you want to apply a filter to a collection of multiple layers, or perhaps save the collection of layers as a new file, while keeping the original layers unchanged and intact.

1   Make sure the layers you want to stamp together are *visible,* and all others are *not* visible.

2   Press Command Option Shift E (PC: Control Alt Shift E).
    All visible layers are combined into one new layer.
    The new layer is placed just above the currently selected layer.
    The original layers remain unchanged.

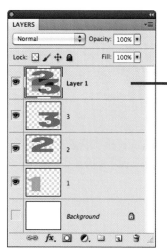

This is the new layer created from the three visible layers. Now I can experiment with applying a filter or effect (below) to this combination layer instead of applying it to three separate layers.

The white Background layer isn't included in the newly stamped layer because its visibility (the eye icon) has been turned off.

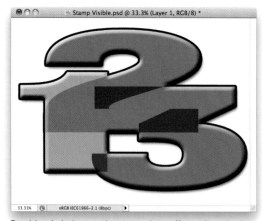

Double-click the new layer to select effects. I applied Drop Shadow, Bevel and Emboss, and Stroke.

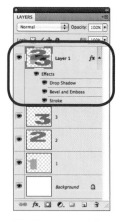

The Layers panel shows applied effects. Click the eye icon to disable any effect.

Group layers to help organize

When a file has a large number of layers, you can stay organized with **Layer Groups.** It's sort of like using folders on your Desktop to keep all your files organized. Keep in mind that *if a layer has a Blending Mode applied that is affected by the layer beneath it, that effect will change if you move either layer.*

To create a Group:

1 Open or create a file with multiple layers.

2 Open the Layers panel.

3 To create a new Group, click the folder icon at the bottom of the panel (circled below). A new Group folder layer appears *above the currently selected layer.* You can move it, of course.

4 Drag layers and drop them into the folder.

5 To change the name of the Group, double-click directly on the layer name.

The Blending Mode for Groups is automatically set to *Pass Through.* This means the group has no blending properties of its own. Layers inside a group that have Adjustment Layers or Blending Modes applied still affect layers below them. However, if you change the Blending Mode for the group, all layers inside the group are treated as a single image and are blended with the rest of the image using the chosen Group Blending Mode. To summarize, most of the time you'll be happy with *Pass Through.*

Label layers with color

You might want to try organizing your layers with **color**. For instance, you might want all your type layers one color, or all the layers with blend modes applied another color, etc.

- Right-click on a layer's visibility icon (the eye icon). From the menu that appears, choose a color.

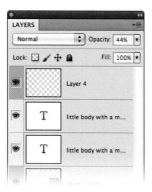

Layer Styles

You can make changes to whole layer at once using a **Layer Style**, which gets applied to everything on that layer—text, shapes, brush strokes, etc. If you add something to the layer later, such as a brush stroke or more text, the new element will display the same style effects. Because you're applying the changes to the layer and not the actual pixels, the changes are *non-destructive;* that is, you can modify or hide these changes at any time without affecting the original image.

1 Double-click the layer to which you want to apply a Layer Style (don't double-click on the name of the layer because that just lets you edit the name).

2 In the "Layer Style" dialog that opens, click on the *name* of a style in the Styles list to show the settings for that style. Click the *checkbox* next to a style name to turn the style on or off.

3 Layer Styles can include multiple settings—experiment with them! When satisfied with the results, click ok. An "fx" symbol appears on the layer to indicate that Layer Styles have been applied to the layer.

The original text layer.

A set of Layer Styles applied to the text layer.

A different set of Layer Styles applied to the text layer.

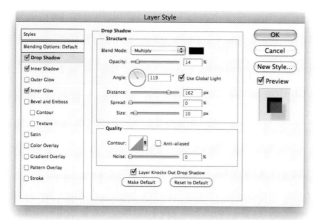

We used these style settings on the example above, right.

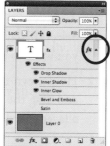

To hide or show the styles, click the small triangle (circled above).

To turn a style on or off, click the eye icon next to the style.

To delete, drag the "fx" to the Trash icon.

TIP: To position a drop shadow, you don't have to use the *Angle* and *Distance* controls in the Layer Style dialog, which can be tedious. Instead, place your cursor over the image in the canvas window and drag the drop shadow to any position you want.

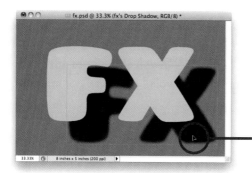

Drag the drop shadow to any position in the document.

See the following pages for more details about Layer Styles.

Adjustment Layers

An Adjustment Layer is a special layer in the Layers panel that applies a filter or effect to the layers below it (the layer itself looks like it has nothing on it, which is how Robin knows it is a magic layer).

Adjustment Layers use the same filters that you can apply using menu commands, but with one very important difference: they leave the original image layer untouched, and you can go back at any time to change the adjustment settings.

1 Open an image to adjust.

2 Open the Adjustments panel: From the Window menu, choose "Adjustments."

3 In the Adjustments panel (below, left), hover over an icon and its function will appear at the top of the panel.

   Single-click an icon to get the controls for that adjustment. To return to the main Adjustments pane, single-click the arrow in the bottom-left corner.

   Or you can choose a preset from the list of presets in the bottom half of the panel—single-click the disclosure triangle to get the options.

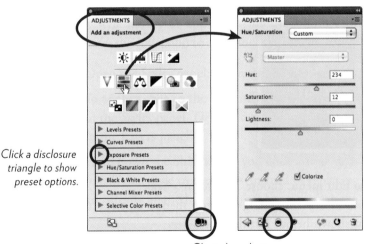

Click a disclosure triangle to show preset options.

Clip to layer buttons.

4 As soon as you select an adjustment, a new layer appears in the Layers panel, the Adjustment Layer, as shown on the opposite page. It appears to have nothing on it, other than an adjustment icon thumbnail and a white mask thumbnail. To modify the adjustment settings, double-click the adjustment icon thumbnail.

5   **Important:** Ordinarily an Adjustment Layer affects *all layers below it.*
    To force the Adjustment Layer to affect *only* the layer *immediately*
    below, click the *Clip adjustment to layer* button, located at the
    bottom of the Adjustments panel. ◉

    The adjustment thumbnail in the Layers panel indents to the right,
    and a small down-pointing arrow appears next to the thumbnail
    (below-right), indicating that the adjustment affects only the
    single layer beneath it. In the example below, the Hue/Saturation
    adjustment removes the color from the subjects in the layer immedi-
    ately below, but ignores the landscape image in the next layer down.

The arrow means the adjustment is "clipped" to the layer beneath and won't affect other layers.

TIP: As shown to the right, another way
to clip an adjustment to the layer below
the Adjustment Layer is to hold down the
Option key (PC: Alt key) and click on the
dividing line between the Adjustment Layer
and the layer below it. When the cursor is
hovered over the dividing line, it changes to
a clipping icon (circled on the right).

To release the clipping so the adjustment affects all layers below,
Option-click (PC: Alt-click) the dividing line again.

To disable clipping, click the button again.

To clip all future adjustment effects, click the *Clip to layer* button
in the bottom-right corner of the general Adjustments panel
(shown opposite, on the left).

To clip only the currently selected Adjustment Layer, click the
Clip to layer button at the bottom of a specific Adjustments panel
(shown opposite, on the right).

Create a Layer Mask

A Layer Mask hides areas of the current layer without harming the image, and reveals the layers below.

This example shows an image of a car hood ornament with a text layer on top. The goal is to make the text *appear* to go behind the wings of the ornament, without harming the text and keeping it editable.

You can create something similar to experiment with—open an image that has an object that text can appear to go behind. Create a new layer with text on it (details about text are in Chapter 6).

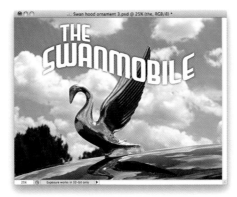

1 Make sure the text layer is above the image layer.
   Select the text layer.

2 From the Layer menu, choose Layer Mask > Reveal All.
   The "Reveal All" part means the mask is filled with white,
   which doesn't hide any of the layer content.

To hide (mask) some of the top layer content (the text) and allow the layer below to show through where text is currently hiding it, you're going to paint black on the mask (but it won't really look black).

3 Single-click on the text thumbnail and lower its Opacity so you can
   see both the text and the ornament where they overlap.

4   Target the Layer Mask (click on its thumbnail, circled below).

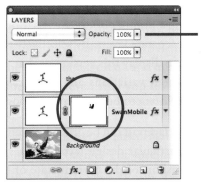

Lower the opacity of a selected layer here. Either: enter a value in the field, or *click on the blue button to get a slider,* or *press-and-drag back and forth on the word "Opacity."*

Set the Foreground color to black, if it isn't already (you can use the shortcut D).

Use a small, hard-edged Brush tool to paint on the mask layer with black, as shown at the bottom of the opposite page. You will see the Brush tool appear to erase the text, and the black paint will appear in the Layer Mask thumbnail, as shown above.

If your brush stroke accidentally masks more of the layer content than you intended, change the foreground color to white, make sure the Layer Mask thumbnail is selected (as above), then paint over the accidental brush strokes. The white paint restores the visibility of the layer content.

5   When you think you've got it, restore the Opacity of the text layer to 100 percent. Et voilà.

If you think you did a crummy job, you can delete the Layer Mask (drag its thumbnail to the Trash icon) and start over. Your text is still all there and editable.

Flatten layers

When you create a file with many layers, it increases the digital size of the file. When you deliver a file to someone, they may want you to flatten the file first so it'll be faster to download and will take less storage space on their computer. Flattening a Photoshop file takes all your layers and combines them into one background layer. Layers that are not currently visible are thrown away. If you do this, be sure to save a copy of the layered file so you can use it for possible future changes.

If your file includes overlapped elements on separate layers, the flattened version of your file will eliminate any part of the image that was hidden by overlapping elements on layers above.

To flatten the layers in a file, open the Layers panel menu (click the tiny menu icon in the upper-right corner of the panel), choose "Flatten Image." The Layers panel menu is shown on page 103.

Make bigger layer thumbnails

You can make the layer thumbnails in the Layers panel larger or smaller, which can be very handy to easily identify the content of various layers, or to economize on how much space the panel takes.

1 From the Layers panel menu, choose "Panel Options."

2 In the "Thumbnail Size" section (right), choose one of the options.

3 Click OK.

Large thumbnails.

Medium thumbnails.

Small thumbnails.

No thumbnails.

Photoshop Type

Type in Photoshop is made from *vector* paths, which are mathematical descriptions of the letterforms. Vector paths let you resize type as much or as often as you want without degrading the quality. All sorts of effects and filters can be applied to type while preserving the ability to edit, scale, rotate, and warp.

Some changes you make to type require that you *rasterize* the type layer, which means Photoshop converts the text to pixels and thus *it is no longer editable as type.* Once you rasterize text, it becomes pixels on the screen, which means you can treat it like any other image in Photoshop, but not as text that you can edit again. **If you need to rasterize your type, make a copy of the original type layer before rasterizing it so you can edit later if necessary.**

Type is always placed on its own layer—a new type layer is automatically created when you click in a document window with the Type tool. As a side benefit, when you forget the name of the font used, you can select the type layer and find the font name in the Character panel.

Type control in Photoshop is fairly robust, but it is designed for special occasions, and is particularly for use in combination with images. That is, if you need crisp, clean typography directly on the paper (instead of on an image) for a letterhead or business card or brochure, a better tool would be either InDesign or Illustrator.

Set type

There are three ways to create type in Photoshop: 1) start at a point (below), 2) create a paragraph (opposite page), and 3) set along a path (see page 124).

Point type

When you have just a few words to set, this is the best way to do it. This method is called "point type" because the text starts at that point and continues along a horizontal path until you hit Return or Enter.

When working with point type, there is no bounding box (see the opposite page) to contain the type, so it will go right off the page! If that happens to you, either move the type (see below) or just click in the text before the point at which it went off the edge, then hit Return or Enter.

1 Select the Horizontal Type tool from the Tools panel.

2 In the Options bar, choose a font and size.

3 Single-click in the canvas window. Photoshop automatically creates a new layer, a type layer for this text.

    Be sure to click in an area that allows your type to move in the proper direction. That is, for English, click on the left side of the window, down far enough to allow the size of the type to appear unobstructed. You can always move it later, but you might as well set it in a position that makes it easy to work with.

this most excellent

← Flashing insertion point. Type moves out from here.

The click point. Text starts here and continues to the right until you hit Return.

This is the baseline. This line disappears when you choose another tool.

- **To move the text**, simply position the cursor outside the area of the type. It automatically and temporarily turns into the Move tool. Drag to move the text.

- **To edit the text later**, choose the Type tool and single-click anywhere in the text. (If the text has been rasterized, you cannot edit it.)

TIP: **Be careful with the Type tool!** Every time you click with the Type tool, Photoshop makes another layer (guess how we know that). If you're not careful, you'll end up with a dozen empty type layers. So as soon as you type your text, choose another tool, a benign one, such as the Rectangular Marquee tool (M).

While you've got the Type tool, you can't use the keyboard shortcut to select another tool—you must actually go to the Tools panel and click on it.

Paragraph type

Setting "paragraph type" is best for larger amounts of text, such as a paragraph or more. It will be contained within a flexible bounding box. Don't worry about the limitations of the bounding box—you can always resize it later.

1   Select the Horizontal Type tool from the Tools panel.

2   Don't click—*press-and-drag* the cursor in the document window to create a boundary for the text; drag diagonally to create a rectangle that's about the size in which you want to contain the text. Photoshop automatically creates a new type layer for this text.

3   Type or paste copy into the boundary shape. If typing, do *not* hit Return or Enter at the ends of the lines—just let them bump into the bounding box edge and the text will continue on the next line.

> I have of late – but wherefore I know not – lost all
> my mirth, forgone all custom of exercise; and
> indeed it goes so heavily with my disposition that
> this goodly frame, the earth, seems to me a sterile
> promontory. This most excellent canopy the air,
> look you, this brave o'erhanging, this majestical
> roof fretted with golden fire – why, it appears no

Text boundary line.

If overflow text doesn't fit within the boundary, a small plus symbol (+) appears in the corner.

The text cursor changes as you move it around a selected text box. The example below shows the different cursors and explains what each does.

❶ **To move the type,** simply move your cursor away from the text, and it temporarily becomes the Move tool. Drag wherever you want.

❷ **To resize the bounding box,** position the cursor directly on top of a handle. When it turns into a double-headed arrow, drag the text box to resize it.

❸ **To tilt the type,** position the cursor just outside any handle until you see the curved double-headed arrow. Drag to tilt.

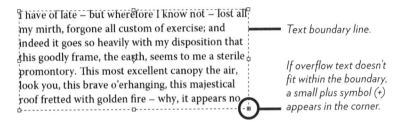

• When you come back to this text layer and want **to edit the text,** simply choose the Type tool and click in the text. The bounding box will appear and you can edit as usual.

• **To deselect the text,** choose a different tool or a different layer.

The Character panel

The Character panel gives you more type options than the Options bar. **To open the Character panel,** go to the Window menu and choose "Character."

The options you choose will apply to whatever is *selected:*

Press Enter to apply a value.

- Click in a document with the Text tool to start setting text, and the options you choose in the Character panel will apply to what you now type (because the flashing insertion point was *selected*).

- *Select* a text layer; the options you choose will apply to all the text on that layer.

- With the Text tool, drag over specific text. The options you now choose will apply to the *selected* characters only.

The **fields of the Character panel** are described below.

Choose a font family and the specific font style within that family.

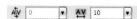

Font size and leading value (leading is the amount of space between lines of text).

*Kerning and tracking. Kerning adjusts the space between a **selected pair** of characters. Tracking adjusts the space between all characters in a **selected range** of text.*

Adjust the vertical or horizontal scale of the type. This distorts the letterforms.

Adjust the baseline shift and type color. Baseline shift refers to how far above or below the baseline (the invisible line upon which type sits) the selected text will set.

T *T* TT Tr T¹ T₁ T T̶

Apply type styles to selected text: Faux (fake) Bold, Faux (fake) Italic, All Caps, Small Caps, Superscript, Subscript, Underline, Strikethrough. (It is always best to choose the family bold or italic style rather than the faux version.)

TIP: Instead of typing numbers in the value fields, position the cursor over the symbol next to the field. When the cursor changes to a hand symbol, drag left or right to change the value in the field.

The Options bar

Or use the Options bar to format text. Make sure the *type layer* and the *Type tool* are selected, and then you'll see these items in the Options bar.

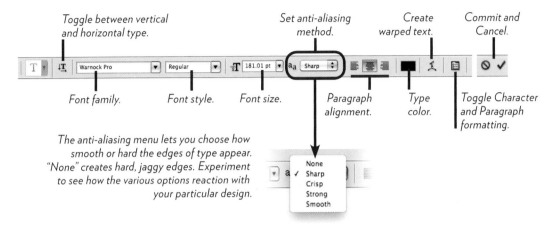

Toggle between vertical and horizontal type.

Set anti-aliasing method.

Create warped text.

Commit and Cancel.

Font family.

Font style.

Font size.

Paragraph alignment.

Type color.

Toggle Character and Paragraph formatting.

The anti-aliasing menu lets you choose how smooth or hard the edges of type appear. "None" creates hard, jaggy edges. Experiment to see how the various options reaction with your particular design.

None
✓ Sharp
Crisp
Strong
Smooth

The Paragraph panel

Paragraph formatting *applies to entire paragraphs,* as opposed to character formatting that applies to individually selected characters. Paragraph formatting includes things like indents, margins, alignments (left, right, centered), space above or below paragraphs, and tabs.

The Paragraph panel provides more controls for paragraph formatting than you'll find in the Options bar.

- **To open the Paragraph panel**, go to the Window menu and choose "Paragraph."

- **To select a paragraph for formatting**, all you need to do is single-click in it with the Text tool, since the options will apply to the whole paragraph whether you like it or not.

- **To select more than one paragraph for formatting**, press-and-drag to select any portion of contiguous (touching) paragraphs.

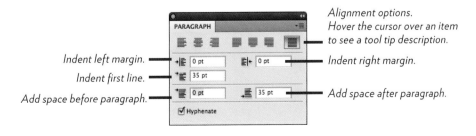

Alignment options.
Hover the cursor over an item to see a tool tip description.

Indent left margin.

Indent first line.

Add space before paragraph.

Indent right margin.

Add space after paragraph.

G
O

S
O
F
T
L
Y

O
N

Vertical text

You've probably noticed there is a Vertical Type tool as well as the horizontal one. This tool stacks your text in a vertical line. Try it. All the formatting features that apply to horizontal text also apply to vertical text.

Change type color

By default, type you create uses the current Foreground color as displayed at the bottom of the Tools panel. You can choose that color *before* you create new type (click in the Foreground color box), or select characters and change the color *after* you type. (See Chapter 11 for more on color.)

To change the color of all text on a certain layer:

1 Select the text layer you want to color.

2 Select the Move tool in the Tools panel. ⊕

3 Click the "Color" swatch in the Character panel, then choose a color from the "Select Text Color" dialog that opens. The text updates immediately with the new selected color.

To change the color of a specific selection of text:

Select the Text tool in the Tools panel and drag to select the specific range of text that you want to color. Then do one of the following:

- From the Window menu, open the Swatches panel or the Color panel and choose (or create) a color.

- Click the Foreground color box at the bottom of the Tools panel, then choose a color from the Adobe Color Picker.

- Click the Color selection box in the Options bar or Character panel. In the "Select text color" dialog that opens, select a color.

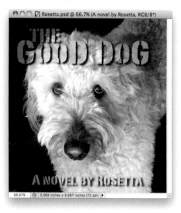

In this example, I applied different colors to individual characters, then chose a layer Blending Mode of "Hard Light." This makes the colors react differently against dark and light backgrounds and allows the image below the text layer to show through.

Specify Smart Quotes

Professional designers use typographer's quotes (" "), also known as curly quotes or smart quotes, instead of straight or typewriter quotes (" ") which look more like inch and foot marks.

1   From the Photoshop menu, choose Preferences > Type.
    PC: from the Edit menu, choose Preferences > Type.

2   In the Type pane, check the box to "Use Smart Quotes."
    Click OK.

Please do *not* use typographer's quotation marks if you are specifying feet and inches. We've seen plenty of bridges with warning signs that say something like **Max. Height 12" 6'**. That's just silly.

Hang the punctuation

Professional typographers and designers always "hang" the punctuation, which forces the punctuation beyond the boundary of the text to create a more consistent margin appearance. If the quotation marks in the first line of a quotation, for instance, make the text appear to be indented, you need to hang it.

1   Select the text layer or the paragraphs you want to affect.

2   From the Paragraph panel menu (single-click the tiny lines in the upper-right corner of the panel), choose "Roman Hanging Punctuation."

Before hanging punctuation.

After hanging punctuation.

Apply effects and styles to text

Photoshop sets type in vector form, as explained on the first page of this chapter, which makes it always editable. As vectors, you can set type on a path or in a shape (see the following pages), adjust its transparency (use the Opacity field in the Layers panel for that layer), apply many transform operations such as scale, skew, and rotate (see Chapter 4). You can even warp text and apply Layer Styles (below).

Warp text

1 Create or select a text layer.

2 Select the Text tool.

3 In the Options bar, single-click the *Create warped text* button.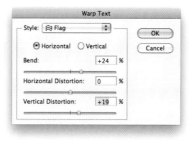

4 From the Style pop-up menu, choose one of the warp options. Select options and adjust sliders to get an effect you like.

5 Click OK.

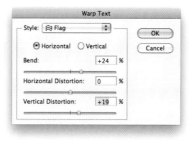

Warped text.

To remove a warp effect, follows Steps 1–3, above. In Step 4, choose "None." Click OK.

Once you rasterize the text, you will not be able to remove the warp!

Apply Layer Styles to text

If you read about Layer Styles in Chapter 5, you might be excited to know that you can apply Layer Styles to text while still maintaining the ability to edit the text later.

1   Select a text layer.

2   From the Layer menu, choose "Layer Style," then choose an effect from the submenu that appears. This opens the "Layer Style" dialog.

　　Or double-click in the blue area of a text layer (not on the *name* of the layer) to open the "Layer Style" dialog.

3   Select from the many styles in the Styles list.
　　Don't just click the little checkbox—single-click the *name* of the style to open its settings. See pages 102–105 for more details about Layer Styles.

We added the Layer Styles called *Drop Shadow, Inner Shadow,* and *Color Overlay* to a warped text layer.

Rasterize the type

There are times when you *must* rasterize the type. For instance, some commands, effects, and tools (such as Vanishing Point, filter effects, and painting tools) will not work on text layers unless the layer is rasterized.

If you try to use a command or apply a filter that requires the type layer to be rasterized, a warning message appears on the screen. The message sometimes includes an ok button you can click to rasterize the layer. If such a button is not provided, go to the Layer menu and choose Rasterize > Type.

Set text on a hand-drawn path

There are times when you want to run type along a curved (but invisible) line. Perhaps you want to follow a curve in a photo or create an arc over a graphic object. Create any path and place text on it. Mmm, that's fun.

1   Draw a path with the Pen tool (below-left). See pages 160–163 if you're not familiar with how the Pen tool works.

2   Select the Text tool in the Tools panel.

3   In the Options bar (below), choose options such as font and alignment before you type. You can always change options settings after you've typed the text (to change the font, font size, or font color of existing text, first use the Text tool to *select* the text, *then* change the settings).

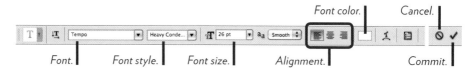

Font color.   Cancel.

Font.   Font style.   Font size.   Alignment.   Commit.

4   If you chose a *left* text alignment, click near the left side of the path with the Text tool, then type. If you chose a *centered* text alignment, click near the center of the path with the Text tool, then type.

5   In the Options bar, click the checkmark icon to commit the text (or any changes you made) and to deselect the text.

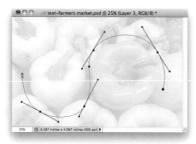

Use the Pen tool to draw a path.

Click the path with the Text tool, then type some text.

Style the text however you want.

In the top two examples I lowered the opacity of the image layer to make the path more visible.

Reposition text on a path

To reposition text on a path, use the Path Selection tool.

1   Select the layer with text on a path. Choose the Path Selection tool.

2   Hover the cursor near the beginning of the text. When the cursor changes to an I-beam-and-triangle as shown above-right, drag the text along the path.

Place text inside or around a shape

You can also put text around or inside shapes created with one of the selection tools or Shape tools.

1   Draw a shape with a selection tool or a Shape tool (see Chapter 10 (we used the Elliptical Marquee tool).

2   Open the Paths panel (right), then click the *Make work path from selection* button at the bottom of the panel.

3   Select the Text tool; click *on* the path to set text along the path but outside of the shape, or *inside* the path to set the type inside the shape.

4   Enter the text you want inside (or outside) the shape.

5   To adjust any of the settings in the Character panel and have it apply to the *entire text layer,* make sure the Move tool is selected in the Tools panel, open the Character panel, and make adjustments.

   To adjust a *specific range of text,* select the text with the Text tool, then make adjustments in the Character panel.

   If necessary, open the Paragraph panel to adjust the paragraph settings.

6   **To hide the path**, select any other layer. To edit the text later, select the text layer, then select the Text tool and click the text. Drag one of the shape's handles to modify the shape.

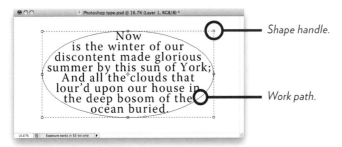

Shape handle.

Work path.

Force type to the inside of a shape

1 Select a layer with text on the edge of a shape. We used a circle drawn with the Elliptical Marquee tool (below left).

2 Drag the Text tool across the text to select it.

3 Open the Character panel and enter a negative number in the Baseline Shift field (left). Lower the Baseline Shift number until the text moves down, across the path, and is aligned with the inside of the shape (below, middle and right). If necessary, in the Character panel, adjust the tracking (the space between letters).

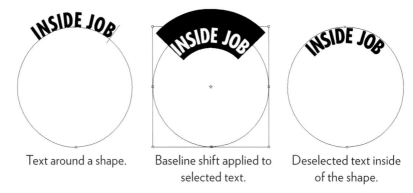

Text around a shape.　　　Baseline shift applied to　　　Deselected text inside
　　　　　　　　　　　　　　　selected text.　　　　　　　of the shape.

Move text to the inside bottom of a circle shape

1 Select a layer with text on the outside of a circle (or other shape).

2 Select the Path Selection tool in the Tools panel and position the cursor over the text.

3 When the cursor changes to an I-beam with double arrows (below left), press-and-drag the text downward until it flips upside down with its baseline aligned with the inside of the circle's path (below middle). Of course that's not what you want, so . . .

4 Continue to drag the text down the side of the shape, all the way to the bottom of the circle, until the text appears upright (below right).

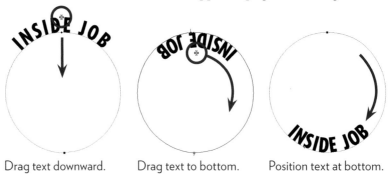

Drag text downward.　　　Drag text to bottom.　　　Position text at bottom.

7 Photoshop with a History

Photoshop is infamous for having one level of Undo. That sounds very limiting (and it is) until you realize the amazing flexibility and forgiveness of the History panel.

The History panel keeps track of every operation you do so you can wander back and forth through your recent Photoshop actions, just like going back in time—and forward again if necessary.

You also have access to the History Brush, which paints on an image using a *former image state* instead of color. It's kind of freaky.

And, of course, the standard Undo, Redo, and Revert commands, though limited, are very useful in any project.

Go back in time . . .

The History panel

The History panel automatically keeps track of everything you do and lets you jump back to previous *states* of the document. The history states are represented by a list of operations in the History panel, shown on the following page. **Click an item in the list and the document changes to how it was at the time of that operation, called its** *state.* Use the History panel as a powerful "Undo" and "Redo" tool, to replace the ordinary "Undo" command (Edit > Undo) that can take you back only one step (state) in the document history.

The number of history states that the History panel stores in memory is determined by your Preferences settings. **To change settings**, go to the Photoshop menu, choose Preferences > Performance (PC: Edit > Preferences > Performance), then use the "History & Cache" pane.

The default number of history states is 20; you can change it to up to 1000, but keep in mind that all of this information is held in memory. When memory gets clogged, it can affect the performance of your entire machine. Unless you have a terabyte of memory installed, keep it to a reasonable number.

- **To preserve different document states while working**, make a *snapshot* of a selected state. Snapshots are temporary and are deleted when you close the document. Open the History panel menu, then choose "New Snapshot…" (below). Snapshots appear above the automatically generated list of states in the panel. You can select a snapshot to revert to that state and continue working from there.

  By default, if you revert back to a previous state and then make changes, or if you delete a state, all states after that are deleted.

- **To avoid deletion of states**, open the History panel menu (below). From "History Options," check the box to *Allow Non-Linear History.*

- **To create a new document from a particular state**, select a history state, open the History panel menu, then select "New Document" (shown on the right).

- **To clear all history states** from the list without changing the image, click the History panel menu, then choose "Clear History."

- **To delete selected history states**, click the History panel menu, then choose "Delete."

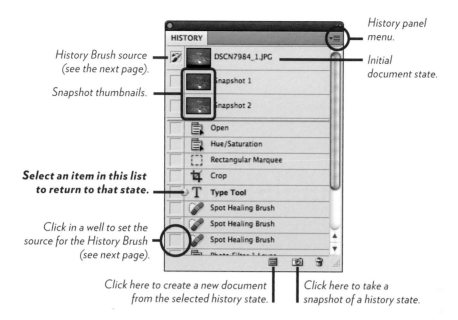

History panel
menu.

History Brush source
(see the next page).

Snapshot thumbnails.

Initial
document state.

**Select an item in this list
to return to that state.**

Click in a well to set the
source for the History Brush
(see next page).

Click here to create a new document
from the selected history state.

Click here to take a
snapshot of a history state.

To specify how many states to show in the History panel, open the History panel menu and choose "History Options…." Select any of these options.

Automatically Create First Snapshot
Automatically creates a snapshot of the image state when the document is opened.

Automatically Create New Snapshot When Saving
Makes a snapshot every time you Save.

Allow Non-Linear History
Make changes to a selected state or delete a state without deleting the states that come after.

Show New Snapshot Dialog
Opens a dialog that prompts you to name your snapshots.

Make Layer Visibility Changes Undoable
Includes layer visibility changes as a recorded step in the history states that appear in the History panel list.

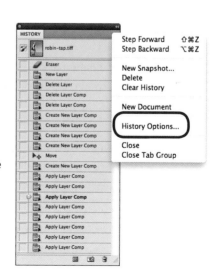

The History Brush tool

The History Brush tool (from the Tools panel) works with the History panel (pages 128–129) to achieve certain effects and restore image elements from previous document history states. The History Brush looks at the History panel to see which document state displays the History Brush icon next to it (shown, left), which designates that state as the History Brush *source*.

The History Brush uses the designated *source* (in the History panel) to paint with. You can change the source as many times as you want and paint with various previous states of the document.

The example below explains one way to use the History Brush.

1 Open a document and make several adjustments to it, such as change the hue or brightness, or apply a filter. We opened a cloud scene, duplicated the layer, and changed the hue to blue.

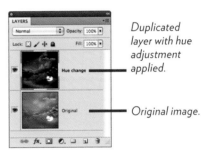

Duplicated layer with hue adjustment applied.

Original image.

The Layers panel above shows the two layers, each with a different hue.

2 From the Window menu, choose "History" to open the History panel (shown below). The number of history states will vary, depending on how much you experimented with filters and other adjustments. The history states shown here indicate we opened the document, duplicated a layer, then made a Hue/Saturation adjustment.

3 In the History panel, select the document state you want to modify (your selection is highlighted in blue).

4 Designate one of the document states as the History Brush *source*: click the well to the left of the state. In this example, the "Open" history state is designated as the source (the image as it looked when it was opened, orange and yellow clouds).

5 Select the History Brush in the Tools panel.

6 Go to the Options bar (below) to specify the brush size, hardness, opacity, and blending mode.

Brush Preset picker. Click to set brush size and hardness.

7 Drag the History Brush across the image where you want to paint with the image as it exists in the selected *source* state.

The History Brush paints with the designated *source* (the document state that used orange and yellow clouds) on top of the *selected* state (the document state that uses the dark blue Hue/Saturation adjustment).

The History Brush is also useful for restoring parts of an image that contain unwanted modifications caused by certain filters or retouching. For example, the image below was distorted using the Liquify filter. The area surrounding the Liquified effect shows unwanted distortion. The History Brush enables you to select a document state before the Liquify filter was used, then paint with that state to restore the area around the distorted element.

The Liquify filter distorted this image, including unwanted background distortion.

The History Brush paints out the distortion by using a previous history state for paint.

Undo, Redo, and Revert

The Undo or Redo commands affect only the most recent actions. If you make a mistake and start clicking around to fix things, all you will Undo is the last click. Try to remember to Undo the very instant you realize you made a boo-boo.

- To undo the last thing you did, from the Edit menu, choose "Undo." The menu gives you a hint as to what you are going to Undo, such as "Undo Typing."

- If you decide that was a mistake, you can undo the Undo command: From the Edit menu, choose "Redo." It will give you a hint as to what you are going to Redo, such as "Redo Typing."

You can always **revert to the last time you saved the file:** From the File menu, choose "Revert." A "Revert" state is added to the History panel, enabling you to return to states *before* the Revert command was applied, if necessary.

The Revert command is disabled if text is selected or if any element is prepared for transformation; that is, if an element is selected and surrounded by a transformation border with handles, as shown below. First commit or cancel the transformation, then try Revert again.

Adjustment Layers

As you know, Photoshop can do amazing things. And chances are, even if you're a Photoshop user, there are some features that you haven't used yet, because you haven't stumbled across them and don't realize how powerful, easy, and convenient they are.

You'll find Adjustment Layers to be invaluable when you want to modify the tonal ranges and color balance of an image (or just part of an image). You'll love how these special layers allow you to make adjustments to an image in a flexible (editable) and non-destructive way; that is, any adjustments you make can be modified or disabled at any time, and they do not affect the original image file.

Get in the habit of using an Adjustment Layer to make changes rather than making them to the image itself—you'll find it comes in handy much more often than you think it might!

Important Adjustment differences

There are two basic ways to access Adjustments—through the Image menu (choose "Adjustments"), and through the Adjustment panels. There is an important difference between the two.

- When you go to the **Image menu** at the top of the screen and use "Adjustments" from there, you permanently alter the image.

- When you use the **Adjustment panels** to create new *Adjustment Layers,* the effects are non-destructive to the original layer (meaning they do *not* permanently alter the image), plus the adjustment settings can be changed at any time in the future.

Adjustments panel

To open the Adjustments panel:

1 Select the layer to which you want to apply adjustments. This is your *target layer.*

 2 Open the Adjustments panel:

  If the Adjustments panel is already in the panels dock on the right side of the screen, single-click its icon.

  If it's not already on the screen, go to the Window menu and choose "Adjustments."

3 Open the Adjustment controls: Single-click an adjustment icon, as shown at the top of the opposite page. This creates an Adjustment Layer in the Layers panel.

  The Adjustment Layer will appear to be blank, but it's actually filled with magic that affects the layer directly beneath. See the following pages for examples.

IMPORTANT: This process automatically creates a new layer directly *above* the layer that you want to affect. So before you create the Adjustment Layer, *make sure to select the layer to which you want the effects to apply.*

In fact, the Adjustment Layer applies to *all* the layers beneath it. If you want the adjustments to apply to only the layer immediately below, click the *Clip to layer* button, located at the bottom of the specific control panel (opposite page, bottom-right).

The icons in the main Adjustments panel (shown below) represent all of the adjustments available as non-destructive Adjustment Layers. Hover over an icon (it turns into a color icon) to display a tool tip that tells you what it is.

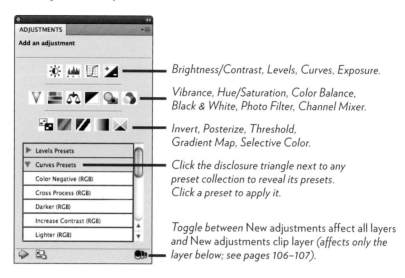

Brightness/Contrast, Levels, Curves, Exposure.

Vibrance, Hue/Saturation, Color Balance, Black & White, Photo Filter, Channel Mixer.

Invert, Posterize, Threshold, Gradient Map, Selective Color.

Click the disclosure triangle next to any preset collection to reveal its presets. Click a preset to apply it.

Toggle between New adjustments affect all layers and New adjustments clip layer (affects only the layer below; see pages 106–107).

When you click one of the adjustment icons (below, left), the settings for that adjustment appear (below, right). To go back to the Adjustments main panel, click the arrow in the bottom-left corner.

Adjustment list and presets.

Levels adjustment panel.

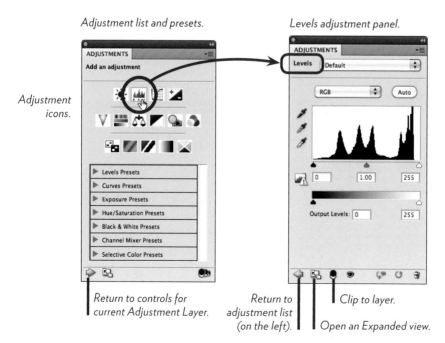

Adjustment icons.

Return to controls for current Adjustment Layer.

Return to adjustment list (on the left).

Clip to layer.

Open an Expanded view.

The Adjustment Layer

The new Adjustment Layer is created just above the target layer (below, left); the target layer is the layer you *select* to affect. The Adjustment Layer contains an adjustment thumbnail that identifies the type of Adjustment Layer it is, and a mask thumbnail (a rectangle) filled with white.

Adjustment Layer.
Adjustment thumbnail.

Target layer.

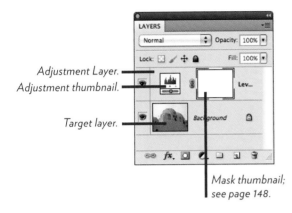

Mask thumbnail;
see page 148.

Once you create the layer (as explained on the previous two pages) and make the adjustments you like (as explained on the following pages), you can always go back and readjust the settings.

- **To modify the existing settings in an Adjustment Layer**, click the adjustment thumbnail in the layer. The Adjustment panel opens to show the current settings. Modify to your heart's content.

- **To delete all those adjustments**, throw away the entire layer— select it in the Layers panel, then click the Trash can icon. *Or* drag the layer to the Trash.

- **To hide the effects of the adjustments**, single-click the eyeball icon to hide the layer and hence its affect on the layer(s) below.

 - **To attach (or clip) the adjustments** to only the layer immediately below the adjustments layer (as opposed to applying to *all* layers beneath), click the *Clip to layer* button at the bottom of the Adjustment Layer, shown on the following page.

The Levels panel

Levels adjusts the balance of highlight, midtone, and shadow values in an image. Do one or more of the following:

- Choose a preset from the uppermost pop-up menu (shown below)

- Click the "Auto" button.

- Adjust the levels manually by sliding the controls under the Histogram.

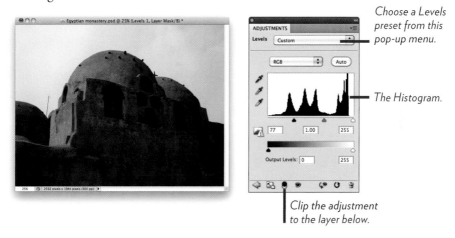

Choose a Levels preset from this pop-up menu.

The Histogram.

Clip the adjustment to the layer below.

- The black triangle in the bottom-left of the Histogram represents shadows, the darker tones. Drag it to the right **to darken dark tones.**

- The white triangle in the bottom-right of the Histogram represents highlights, the lighter tones. Drag it to the left **to lighten the highlights.**

- The gray triangle in the middle of the Histogram represents midtones. Drag it left or right **to lighten or darken midtones.**

- Use the **eyedropper tools** to adjust the levels:

   Select the black eyedropper tool and click on the darkest area of the image. This is called "setting the black point."

   Select the white eyedropper tool and click on the lightest part of the image (called "setting the white point").

   This should automatically set the midtone values, but you can manually adjust the midtones if necessary: select the gray eyedropper and click a midtone area of the image.

The Brightness/Contrast panel

Brightness/Contrast adjusts brightness and contrast, but because it applies to all pixels arbitrarily, it provides less control than using *Levels* (previous page) or *Curves* adjustments (below).

The Curves panel

Curves can be used to adjust highlights, midtones, and shadows of the entire image or of individual color channels. Choose a preset from the uppermost pop-up menu, *or* click the "Auto" button. For more control, choose "RGB" (or a specific color channel) in the pop-up menu, then do the following:

> Select the *Target Adjustment Tool* (circled, right), then press-and-drag up or down in areas where you want to adust the tonal values. The *Curves* graph reacts as you drag the cursor around the image.

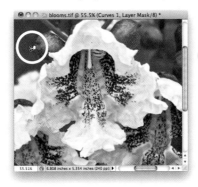
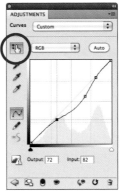

The Exposure panel

Exposure adjusts tonality, primarily for HDR images (High Dynamic Range). An HDR image combines several exposures of the same image and uses the best parts of each exposure. The *Exposure* adjustments can be used with both regular images from your camera and those that were originally shot in HDR.

Drag the sliders to adjust the image. Or use the Eyedropper tools to set black and white points: click on a dark tone in the image with the black Eyedropper tool to set the darks, click a light tone with the white eyedropper tool to set the white point. All tones between are adjusted automatically.

The Vibrance panel

"Saturation" refers to how soaked with color a hue is, how intense it is. The *Vibrance* slider adjusts the saturation of less saturated colors more than colors that are already saturated. It also protect skintones from being over saturated. The *Saturation* slider saturates all colors equally.

The Vibrance slider adds color saturation without over-saturating colors that are already highly saturated. The +100 Vibrance setting above saturates the color in the white flower petals.

The Color Balance panel

Color Balance adjusts the overall balance of the color in an image. Adustments can be made for shadows, midtones, and highlights.

1   Select a tonal range to adjust: Shadows, Midtones, or Highlights.

2   Drag the color sliders to experiment with settings.

3   Check the *Preserve Luminosity* option to prevent the adjustment from darkening the image.

In the image above, we adjusted the color balance of the highlights to have a yellow cast.

The Hue/Saturation panel

Hue/Saturation adjusts hue (color), saturation (intensity), and lightness of an image. The "Colorize" option creates sepia tone and duotone effects.

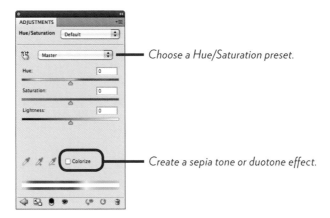

Choose a Hue/Saturation preset.

Create a sepia tone or duotone effect.

To globally change the hue or saturation of an image:

- Choose a preset from the uppermost pop-up menu in the panel, the one currently set to "Default."

- Or drag the Hue and Saturation sliders left or right.

The Hue/Saturation Adjustment Layer desaturates the image below it. The black paint on the image layer mask hides the desaturation in the lamp area.

The original image.   Saturation adjusted.

To change the hue or saturation of a specific color range within the image:

- Select a preset color range from the pop-up menu that is usually set to "Master" (shown at the top of the page), then drag the Hue and Saturation sliders.

To make Hue/Saturation adjustments that are specific to the colors in the current image:

1 Select the *Targeted Adjustment tool* icon in the Hue/Saturation panel (circled, below right).

2 Move the tool over colors in the image you want to adjust—the cursor changes to an eyedropper. Click to sample (select) the color range you want to effect.

3 Now press-and-drag left or right in the image to adjust the **saturation** of the sampled color range (the cursor changes to the *Targeted Adjustment tool* icon, shown below).

   To adjust the **hue** of the sampled color range, hold down the Command key (PC: Control key) as you drag left or right.

Reset adjustment.

The original image.

Command-drag (PC: Control-drag) the Targeted Adjustment tool to modify the hue of the sampled color range.

—continued

You can also use the Eyedropper tools (shown below) in the *Hue/Saturation* panel to select a color range to adjust.

1   To activate the Eyedropper tools, choose any color from the pop-up menu shown as "Master" (below, right).

2   Select the first of the three Eyedropper tools. The other two Eyedropper tools can be used to add to the selected color range, or subtract from it.

3   Single-click on a color in the image you want to adjust (yellow, in this example).

4   Drag the Hue and/or Saturation sliders.

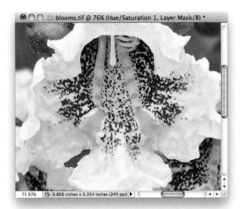 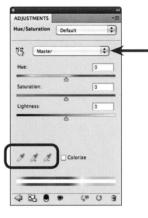

Before the Hue adjustment.

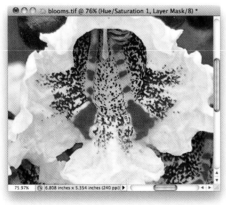 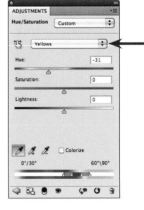

After the Hue adjustment.

The Channel Mixer panel

Channel Mixer creates grayscale or tinted images.

To create a grayscale conversion:

1 Select one of the grayscale presets from the uppermost pop-up menu, next to "Channel Mixer."

2 Experiment, if you want, with the color sliders to affect the grayscale values in the image.

3 Adjust the "Constant" slider to lighten or darken the image.

To create a tinted effect:

1 Select one of the grayscale presets from the uppermost pop-up menu, next to "Channel Mixer."

2 Deselect the "Monochrome" checkbox.

3 Drag the color sliders to add a color tint to the image.

   Also, experiment with changing the "Output Channel" pop-up menu to red, blue, or green, then adjusting the sliders. Although it can be baffling to adjust colors using the RGB (Red Green Blue) color space, you'll get used to it, and will probably stumble across some effects you wouldn't have imagined.

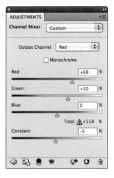

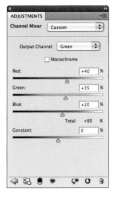

The Photo Filter panel

Photo Filter adds casts of color to an image, similar to the effect of using a color filter on a camera.

- Choose a filter color from the *Filter* pop-up menu, *or* select the *Color* button and click the well to choose a custom color.
- Adjust the *Density* slider to adjust the strength of the color.
- Select *Preserve Luminosity* to prevent the effect from darkening the image.

The Posterize panel

Posterize converts an image to a limited number of flat colors for a silkscreened poster effect. Drag the *Levels* slider to set the number of colors to use.

The Black & White panel

Black & White is another way to convert a color image to grayscale, with more control than the automatic black-and-white conversion that results from going to the Image menu and choosing Mode > Grayscale.

- The uppermost pop-up menu provides preset options that you can choose, *or* you can select the "Auto" button.

- For more control, single-click the *Targeted Selection Tool* icon (circled below), then press-and-drag in areas of the image that you want to adjust. The color sliders react as you drag inside the image.

- To tint the image with control, check the *Tint* checkbox and adjust the sliders. Everything is a matter of experimentation!

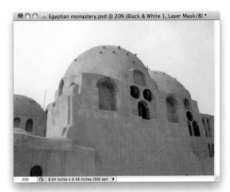 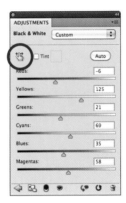

The Invert panel

Invert reverses the colors in an image, without providing any control other than the flexibility to turn the effect on or off in the Layers panel, as you can with any Adjustment Layer.

The Threshold panel

Threshold converts grayscale or color images to high-contrast black-and-white images. Drag the slider under the graph to set a *Threshold* level.

 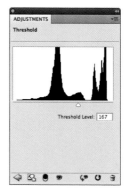

The Gradient Map panel

Gradient Map maps the grayscale range of an image to the colors of a selected gradient. You might want to experiment with this adjustment to create a special effect using different gradients.

- Click the *Gradient Fill* pop-up to choose a preset gradient.
- Single-click the gradient bar to make endless adjustments to the current gradient, to add more gradients, to name them, etc.
- Select the *Dither* option if you want to add noise and reduce color banding.
- Select the *Reverse* option if you want to reverse the effect of the gradient.

Not for every project, but interesting.

The Selective Color panel

Designers love to tinker with images. We assume any photo can be improved or made more interesting. That includes making all sorts of color adjustments. *Selective Color* adjusts the amount of process color (CMYK, the color mode used for high-quality printing) in a specified primary color without affecting other primary colors. You can adjust various colors, all differently, and each will have its own layer for readjusting or eliminating.

From the "Colors" pop-up menu, choose the color range you want to adjust. Experiment with the "Relative" or "Absolute" options, which give slightly different results depending on the colors in the image.

We adjusted the reds in this image (the bricks and pot).

Auto Adjustments

Even though non-destructive techniques such as Adjustment Layers are a good practice, you don't have to use them. If it's okay with you that the original image is altered forever, go to the Image menu, choose "Adjustments," then from the submenu (right) choose the type of adjustment you want to make. Or choose one of the Auto adjustments in the Image menu: Auto Tone, Auto Contrast, or Auto Color. These automatic adjustments don't provide any controls, but often they are all you need to improve an image.

Adjustment masks

When you create an Adjustment Layer, the layer contains a thumbnail icon that represents the type of adjustment you chose, and also a **Layer Mask thumbnail** filled with white. When the mask is filled with white, any layer adjustments you make are fully visible on the layer below. In most cases, you will probably ignore the mask altogether, but it can be very useful if you want to hide (mask) the effects of the adjustment in different parts of the image. In the example below, we've added a lot of contrast to the image by darkening it (using a Levels Adjustment Layer), then masking/hiding the dark effect in selected parts of the image.

1   Open an image that appears flat and needs more contrast.

 2   Add a Levels Adjustment Layer: From the Window menu, choose "Adjustments." Click the Levels icon in the Adjustments panel.

A new Adjustment Layer appears in the Layers panel (below, left). In the Levels panel, drag the left triangle under the histogram to the right to darken the image.

3   Set default colors for the Foreground (black) and Background (white): press D.

4   Click the *mask thumbnail* in the Adjustment Layer to select it.

5   Select the Brush tool from the Tools panel.

6   In the Options bar, click the Brush Preset picker to choose a large brush size and low hardness setting. Paint on the main image (not in the tiny thumbnail) in areas where you want to *hide* the darkened adjustment effect. Where you paint with black, the lightness of the original image shows; these black strokes are visible in the mask thumbnail, but not on the image! Shades of gray in the mask thumbnail indicate a partially masked area, as seen in the soft transition from light to dark, created by a soft brush edge.

You can also adjust the opacity of the Adjustment Layer.

Levels adjustment icon.

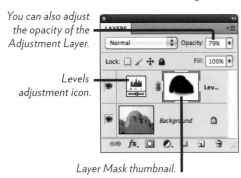

Layer Mask thumbnail.

9 Working with Transparency

All layers, except Background layers, are transparent. Even if a layer is filled with pixels, such as an image, a fill color, or both, the layer itself retains transparency capabilities, allowing other layers below it to show through when pixels on the top layer are erased or masked.

You can give any layer a degree of transparency by adjusting its opacity. Whenever necessary, the Background layer can be converted from a non-transparent layer to a regular transparent layer.

Transparent layers are what provide the remarkable flexibility and creative potential of Photoshop—it's important to understand how they're working for you!

The checkerboard area indicates where this image is transparent.

The transparent area allows the image on another layer to show through onto this layer.

149

What is transparency?

With the exception of "Background" layers (which are not transparent), image layers consist of opaque pixels against a transparent background. The transparent areas of a layer are represented by a gray and white checkerboard pattern. In the example below, the layer of Jimmy and Scarlett is *above* a layer that contains an image of flower blooms. Where the background of the top layer is erased (where you see the checkerboard), the flower bloom layer can show through. In addition, layer opacity can be adjusted to any degree of transparency, which opens up all sorts of visual effects possibilities.

A partially erased layer that does not have another layer below it.

A layer's background erased to reveal the layer below it.

The Layers panel shows the transparency of both layers.

Transparency preferences

Photoshop's preferences allow you to decide how you want to be reminded that a layer is transparent, via a checkerboard grid (or not).

1 From the Photoshop menu, choose Preferences > Transparency & Gamut… (PC: Edit > Preferences > Transparency & Gamut…).

2 From the pop-up menu, choose a preset *Grid Size* and *Grid Colors* for the transparency checkerboard. To create custom grid colors, click the color swatches (shown below).

   To hide the transparency checkerboard, choose "None" for *Grid Size*.

3 Click OK.

These two colors make the transparency checkerboard. Click a color to change it.

Lock the transparent pixels

When a layer contains both an image *and* areas of transparency, you can protect the transparent areas while you edit the image. For example, you might have an element on a layer, such as handlettering (shown below) that you want to add brush strokes to, without letting the brush strokes touch the background area. Locking the transparency enables you to do that. Photoshop refers to transparent areas as "transparent pixels," so when we say "Lock transparent pixels," we mean lock the transparency so that it's protected and preserved.

1 Create a new layer: click the *Create new layer* icon at the bottom of the Layers panel. *Or* from the Layer menu, choose New > Layer….

2 Select the Brush tool and paint a word on the layer, as shown below.

Lock transparent pixels.

Visibility for this layer is turned off.

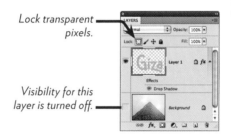

3 Click the *Lock transparent pixels* icon (called-out above).

4 Choose a darker paint color, then brush across the layer to add brush strokes on top of the word. Because the transparent pixels are locked, the new color you paint does not affect the transparent areas, just the visible ones.

I wrote the word *Giza* with a brush on a transparent layer. Then I locked the transparent area and brushed with abandon over the word. The new color did not affect the locked transparent area.

For the final version, I added a drop shadow layer style and turned on the bottom layer visibility.

Lock image pixels and position

There are four "Lock" icons in the Layers panel; the first one is explained on the previous page. The other three Lock icons affect layer transparency in these ways:

- *Lock Image Pixels* prevents visible pixels on the layer from being altered in any way.

- *Lock Position* prevents visible pixels from being moved.

- *Lock All* locks transparent pixels and pixel position (the visible image pixels can't be moved or altered in any way).

When a layer is **partially locked** (when just one or two of the "Lock" items are selected), a white lock icon is shown on the layer (below-left).

When a layer is **fully locked** (when the "Lock All" icon is selected), a black lock icon is shown on the layer (below-right).

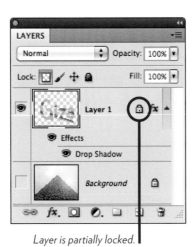

Layer is partially locked.

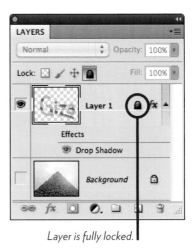

Layer is fully locked.

You can unlock the transparent pixels of a selected layer at any time in order to work in the transparent areas of the layer.

Use the Fill setting for special effects

While the *Opacity* setting in the Layers panel determines how transparent everything on the layer is, the *Fill* setting, also in the Layers panel, affects only pixels, shapes, or text. It does *not* affect the opacity of layer effects that you've applied, such as drop shadows, bevel & emboss, stroke, etc.

With the layer fill set to 0%, everything on the layer is transparent except the layer style, a drop shadow.

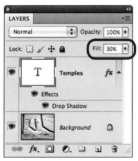  

This layer fill is set to 30%.

Fill image pixels with color

To color the image pixels on a transparent layer with the current **Foreground** color, without locking the transparency: Select the layer, then press Option Shift Delete (PC: Alt Shift Backspace).

To color the image pixels on a transparent background with the current **Background** color: Select the layer, then press Command Shift Delete (PC: Control Shift Backspace). This is similar to "Lock transparent pixels" on page 151.

153

Change Background layer opacity

The opacity of a Background layer cannot be changed; you must convert the Background to a regular (transparent) layer. Do one of the following:

- Double-click the Background layer; click OK.
- Drag the Background layer's lock icon to the Trash icon.
- From the Layer menu, choose New > Layer From Background…; click OK.

Save as TIFF with transparency

You can save an image as a file that preserves its transparency to maximize design choices when it's placed in a page layout application such as InDesign.

1 From the File menu, choose Save As….

2 In the "Save As" dialog, set "Format" as TIFF.

3 Deselect the "Layers" option, to make the file smaller.

4 Choose a name and location for the file, then click "Save."

5 In the TIFF Options dialog (below), check "Save Transparency."

6 Place the TIFF file in InDesign and enjoy the design freedom of working with a transparent background image.

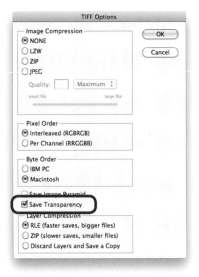

A transparent background provides the design option to overlap one image file on top of another in an InDesign project, as shown above.

10 Draw & Paint

Photoshop is not just an image *editing* application— it's also an image *creation* tool. With the draw and paint tools, you can create just about anything you can imagine.

Learn how to create vector shapes (mathematically based), or rasterized shapes (pixel based), depending on the mode you choose. Photoshop provides customizable libraries of individual shapes to play with and a large variety of customizable brushes to paint with.

Use a pressure-sensitive digital tablet, if possible. Photoshop brushes can react to pen pressure, angle, and rotation as you draw with them.

The versatile drawing and painting tools presented in this chapter will provide new solutions and creative opportunities for your projects.

Draw with shapes from shape libraries, or create your own custom shape libraries.

Customize any paint brush and modify its settings, or choose from a large collection of preset brushes.

Create "elbows" (LBOs: lines, boxes, ovals)

Photoshop is such a sophisticated program that it can be difficult to figure out how to draw simple shapes, such as lines, boxes, and ovals (affectionately called *elbows*). If you're accustomed to InDesign or Illustrator, you'll be looking for the rectangle or ellipse tool, but there isn't one in Photoshop.

Here is the quick and easy way to draw boxes and ovals. But remember that these are *raster* images, pixel based, which means you can erase pieces of them with the Eraser tool, but you can't click on the shapes as objects to change their fill colors or borders. (To create vector shapes, see pages 158 and 164–169.)

To draw a rectangle, square, oval, or random shape and fill it with color:

1 Choose one of the selection marquee tools, such as the Rectangle Marquee, Elliptical Marquee, any of the Lasso tools, or even the Quick Selection tool or Magic Wand.

2 Create a shape with the tool.

3 While the "marching ants" are visible (the moving border), fill the shape:

> **To fill the shape with the Foreground color,** press Option Delete (PC: Alt Backspace).

> **To fill the shape with the Background color,** press Command Delete (PC: Control Backspace)

To add a color border (called a *stroke*) around a raster shape:

1 Follow Steps 1 and 2, above, to create the shape.

2 While the "marching ants" are visible, create the border:
   Go to the Edit menu and choose "Stroke…."

3 Enter a pixel width.
   Click the color well to choose a color.
   Choose where you want the border located.
   If you want a blending mode applied or a lower opacity, choose it.
   Click OK.

To turn off the selection marquee:

> Press Command D (PC: Control D).

To draw a single pixel line across the entire document:

1 Choose the Single Row Marquee tool or the Single Column Marquee tool.

2 Single-click where you want the line to appear, and drag the mouse to move the line.

3 Fill the line with color and/or stroke it as explained on the opposite page. See an example on page 74.

To draw a line in any direction, use the Line Tool, found in the Custom Shapes Option bar (shown at the bottom of page 158). See pages 164–169 about vector shapes. You can also use the Pen tool to create a path; see pages 160–163.

Change the colors with the Paint Bucket tool

You can use any of the techniques throughout this book to change the colors just as you would adjust the colors in a photograph. Or use the **Paint Bucket tool**, one of Robin's favorites because it reminds her of SuperPaint. The paint pours from the one tiny pixel at the end of the spilling paint in the icon.

1 Get the Paint Bucket (it's usually hiding under the Gradient tool).

2 In the Options bar, choose whether you want the fill to be the foreground color or a pattern. If foreground, choose your color in the Foreground swatch at the bottom of the Tools panel; if pattern, choose a pattern from the Pattern well in the Options bar (add more patterns by clicking the tiny triangle in the corner of that panel).

3 Also in the Options bar, choose a blending mode, if you like, and the opacity.

    The "Tolerance" tells the Paint Bucket whether to replace *only* the colored pixels that match *and* are touching the pixel you click on (tolerance of 0), or to spread out to similar colors (higher tolerance).

    Check "Contiguous" if you want the paint to apply only to pixels that are *touching* the one you pour into.

    Uncheck "Contiguous" if you want to replace all items of the pixel color the tool touches, even if the elements are not touching.

    Check "All layers" if you want the Paint Bucket to replace all matching colors on all visible layers.

4 Then pour into any contained shape, even if it's already a color.

Drawing with shapes and pens

In Photoshop's drawing tools, you have a choice between drawing lines of varying widths and colors, drawing geometric shapes that you can customize, and using pre-made custom shapes from a library. With these drawing tools, you can choose to create **pixel-based shapes using the *Fill pixels* mode** (opposite page) or **vector-based shapes that are eternally editable using the Shape layers mode** (see pages 164–169). Be sure you choose the mode that is appropriate for what you want to accomplish.

You can also use the **Pen tool** and the **Freeform Pen tool**; with the Pen tools you can create custom shapes (in the form of *paths*). You can fill these paths and change the fill at any time (you can stroke the shape, but you have to rasterize the shape first, which means you cannot adjust it later).

Before you draw:

1   Select a Shape tool or a pen tool.

> The **Shape tools** are in the pop-out menu along with the Rectangle tool, as shown below, left.

> The **Pen tools** (the regular Pen tool and the Freeform Pen tool) are grouped together, as shown below, right.

Shape tools   Pen tools (and accessories)

2   When you select a tool, the Options bar displays new options, as shown below. Choose one of three drawing modes: *Shape layers, Paths,* or *Fill pixels,* depending on what you want to do. Each mode is explained on the following pages.

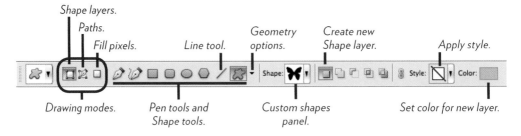

Shape layers.
Paths.
Fill pixels.
Line tool.
Geometry options.
Create new Shape layer.
Apply style.

Drawing modes.   Pen tools and Shape tools.   Custom shapes panel.   Set color for new layer.

Draw a shape in *Fill pixels* mode

The *Fill pixels* mode creates raster images, not vector graphics. That means you cannot enlarge the shapes later without loss of quality, and the editing changes you can make are limited.

1 Create a new layer, *or* select an existing layer (not the Background) that is not vector-based.

2 Select a Shape tool, as shown on the opposite page.

3 Select the *Fill pixels* icon in the Options bar.

4 Select a foreground color.

5 Shapes are pixel-based and behave like other raster images, so set the options in the Options bar *before* you draw (because you can't change these *after* you've drawn the shapes, as you can with vectors). The options change depending on which tool you choose:

> **Shape:** If you choose the Custom Shape tool, you can click here to choose a shape from the library.
>
> **Mode:** Controls how the shape color interacts with other colors.
>
> **Opacity:** Determines how transparent the shape will be.
>
> **Anti-alias:** Smooths the pixels on the edges and blends them with surrounding pixels.

Set additional tool-specific options, such as the number of **sides** for the Polygon tool, the **radius** on the corner of the Rectangle Shape tool, or the **weight** (width in pixels) for the Line tool.

6 *Now* you can draw a shape on the currently selected layer. You can draw multiple shapes on the same layer, but remember that once they overlap each other, changes are difficult and sometimes impossible. (You'll have more flexibility if you draw each shape on a separate layer.)

These three speech balloons (from the Shape library using the Custom Shape tool; see pages 164–165) are drawn on the same layer. I chose the color, opacity, and mode before drawing each one.

Because they are pixel-based, I cannot change the shapes at all, and changing the colors will be tricky. I can, however, erase pixels or paint over them or select pieces and move them. Anything you can do to a photograph, you can do to these drawn pixels.

Draw a shape with the Pen tool

Use the Pen tool to manually draw a shape and fill it. Choose the Pen tool, and in the Options bar, click the *Shape layers* button.

If you know how to use the Pen tool in Illustrator and InDesign, you'll find this one in Photoshop to be very similar. If you've never used a Pen tool before (it is *really* different from any other tool), follow the simple directions below. If you want to learn more about the Pen tool, experiment with the directions on the next three pages.

To experiment with the Pen tool, first draw a random shape with **straight lines.**

1 Open a blank document so it's easy to see the path you draw.

2 For now, choose white for the foreground color (shortcut: tap the letter D, then tap the letter X to choose white as the foreground).

3 Select the Pen tool from the Tools panel.

4 Single-click anywhere—a point appears (shown below).

Single-click somewhere else—a *path* connects the two click points.

Continue to single-click. You're creating a path made of straight lines with tiny squares at the corners. The squares are called *corner points.*

5 **To complete the shape**, single-click directly on the first point.

Photoshop created a new Shape layer in the Layers panel for you that includes Color Fill and Vector Mask thumbnails (see page 164).

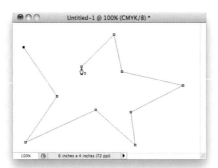

When you hover over the first point, a small circle appears that indicates the path will be closed (completed) when you click on that point.

To change the fill color, double-click the Color Fill thumbnail in the Layers panel. This opens a color picker; choose a color. Click ok.

To stroke (border) this shape, you have to rasterize the layer first (which means you won't be able to adjust the path anymore): Right-click on the layer and choose "Rasterize Layer" from the menu that pops up. From the Edit menu, choose "Stroke…." Choose the width and a color. Click ok.

TIP: If you prefer **freeform drawing** instead of setting specific points, use the **Freeform Pen tool.** Draw on the screen as if it's a regular pen; points and control handles are created automatically. Ultimately, however, the regular Pen tool provides more precise control.

Once you learn to control the Pen tool and its points and handles, you'll find it extremely useful.

To make a curved path using a smooth point:

1   Curved lines come out of *smooth points* (although the tiny squares look the same whether they are smooth points or corner points).

Don't *click* with the Pen tool, but *press-and-drag.* You'll see a *control handle* pull out of the point where you started. The length and direction of these control handles determine the path's curve.

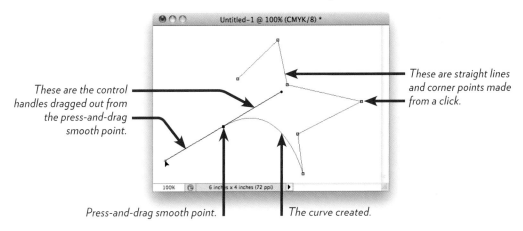

These are the control handles dragged out from the press-and-drag smooth point.

These are straight lines and corner points made from a click.

Press-and-drag smooth point.   *The curve created.*

2   Press-and-drag the next several points to experiment. Control the curves by how far and in which direction you stretch the control handles before you let go.

(As you draw a curved path with smooth points, you can switch to creating a corner point: Single-click the next point instead of dragging a handle out of it.)

3   To complete the path, single-click the first point in the path.

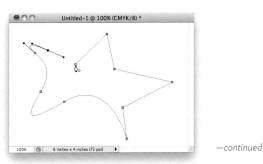

I used smooth points to create the path on the left side of the star.

—continued

As mentioned on the previous page, you can switch back and forth from creating corner points to smooth points as you draw.

You can also **change the type of point you just created.** For example, if you dragged a handle out of a point to create a curve, but now you want the path to change directions *abruptly* from that smooth point to the next point, do this:

Hold down the Option key (PC: Alt key) and single-click the existing point that has handles coming from it (circled below).

This changes the identity of the point from a *smooth point* to a *hybrid point.* The path still curves gracefully into that point, but the control handle exiting out of the point to control the next segment is gone. The next point you click makes the path come straight out of that point, instead of curving out. This means you can adjust the control handles on the curved segment without affecting the line coming out from that point. (That sounds confusing, but experiment with it and you'll get used to it.)

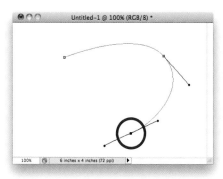

Press-and-drag to create smooth points, then Option-click (PC: Alt-click) the last-drawn point to change it to a corner point.

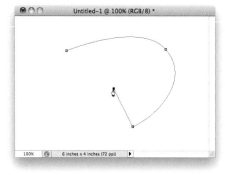

The next click sends the path straight out of the point, instead of curving out. You won't have a control handle on that side of the point.

A GOOD EXERCISE: On one layer, type a 120-point letter D with low opacity. On a layer above this D, use the Pen tool to recreate that shape, directly on top of the letter. Once you get that down, try the letters S and G. By then you'll be an expert.

To move or modify points in a path after the path is completed, use the path Selection tools. Use the white arrow, the Direct Selection tool, to select and manipulate *individual* points and lines. Use the Path Selection tool, the black arrow, to select, manipulate, move, and delete the *entire group* of points as an object. Experiment with paths and points until you feel comfortable.

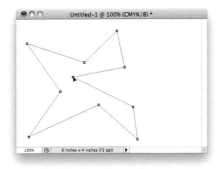

- **To display all the points** if they're not showing, get the Direct Selection tool (the white arrow) and click anywhere on a line.

- **To select a specific point in a path**, single-click the point with the Direct Selection tool (the white arrow).

- **To move an existing point**, get the Direct Selection tool (the white arrow). Drag any point to a new position.

- **To change a curve**, with the Direct Selection tool (white arrow), single-click on a point so it shows its handles. Drag one of the *handles* coming out of the point.

- **To select multiple points**, use the Direct Selection tool (white arrow). Hold down the Shift key after selecting the first point, then click on additional points, *or* press-and-drag around the line to select points.

- **To deselect a point**, hold down the Shift key and single-click on it with the Direct Selection tool (white arrow).

- **To select an entire path**, click it with the Path Selection tool (the black arrow). This lets you move the entire path as an object, apply transformations, delete the entire path all at once, etc.

- **To change a point from a corner point to a smooth point**, get the Convert Point tool (it's under the Pen tool). Press-and-drag a point.

- **To toggle** between the Path Selection tool (black arrow) and the Direct Selection tool (white arrow), hold down the Command key (PC: Control key). Let go to keep the current tool.

- **To fill a shape with color and add a stroke** (outline), see page 160.

—continued

Draw shapes in *Shape layers* mode

When you create a shape in *Shape layers* mode, Photoshop automatically creates a new layer that includes a Color Fill thumbnail and a Vector Mask thumbnail on the same layer:

This is the new layer. The red square is the **Color Fill thumbnail.**

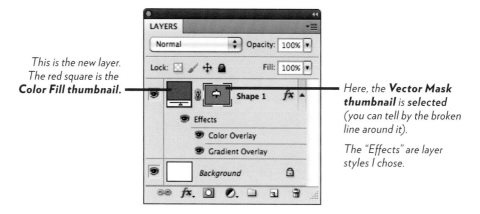

Here, the **Vector Mask thumbnail** *is selected (you can tell by the broken line around it).*

The "Effects" are layer styles I chose.

You can change the fill (inside) color, or you can fill the shape with a gradient or a pattern, edit the shape's vector mask to modify the shape, or apply layer styles to the layer. You can come back next year and make all these changes because it is a *vector* object (as opposed to a *raster* object).

To experiment, use the **Custom Shape tool** to create a *Shape layer.*

1 Select the Custom Shape tool from the Tools panel. As soon as you select the tool, the Options bar displays the Shape options, as shown below.

2 In the Options bar, single-click the *Shape layers* drawing mode.

3 In the Options bar, single-click the *Create new shape layer* icon.

4 Single-click the *Custom shapes* icon to open its panel (next page).

Shape layers.   *Custom Shape tool.*   *Create new Shape layer.*

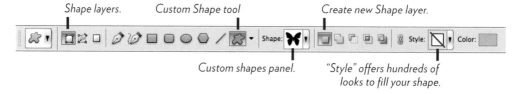

Custom shapes panel.   *"Style" offers hundreds of looks to fill your shape.*

5 Choose a custom shape to draw with. If you don't see a shape you want, click the small triangle in the top-right corner of the panel to "append" (add) other Shape libraries to the panel.

6 From the Options bar, choose a "style" (if you want one) and "color."

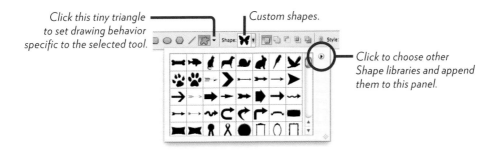

Click this tiny triangle to set drawing behavior specific to the selected tool.

Custom shapes.

Click to choose other Shape libraries and append them to this panel.

7   With a shape selected, press-and-drag in the document window to draw the shape (shown below).

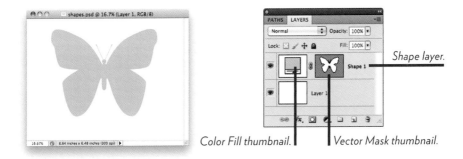

Shape layer.

Color Fill thumbnail.   *Vector Mask thumbnail.*

A new Shape layer is created for every shape you draw *unless* you choose one of the other options to the right of the *Create new shape layer* icon. These include *Add to shape area, Subtract from shape area, Intersect shape areas,* and *Exclude overlapping shape areas.* Experiment with how they interact as you create shapes on top of each other.

To change the fill color, single-click the vector mask thumbnail in the layer (see the callout above) to select it. Now click the "Color" swatch in the Options bar and select a color. You can also change the "style." **To deselect the vector mask,** click its thumbnail again.

To reshape the object, select the vector mask. Choose the Direct Selection tool (the white arrow). Click on the object to make the points and handles appear, then drag them (see pages 161–163).

To move all shapes on the layer, select the Move tool (V) and drag.

To move individual shapes, choose the Path Selection tool (the black arrow), single-click on the shape to select it, and drag.

Change the Color Fill of a shape

If you originally drew the shape with a "style" attached to it (see page 164), you must first select the vector mask (single-click on it) and change the "style" to "None." Otherwise you won't see the color fill change. For regular vector shapes with no "style," it's very simple:

1 Double-click the Color Fill thumbnail in the Layers panel (shown below, left).

2 In the Color Picker that opens (below, right), choose a different color.

Double-click the Color Fill thumbnail to open the Color Picker (right).

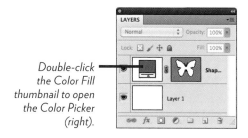
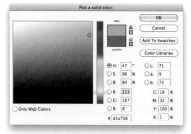

Fill a shape with a gradient or pattern

1 Draw a vector-based shape in the *Shape layers* mode (see pages 164–165). A Shape layer is added to the Layers panel.

2 Select the Shape layer in the Layers panel.

3 From the Layer menu, choose Layer Style > Gradient Overlay….

4 In the Layer Style dialog that opens (below left), click the "Gradient" swatch to choose a gradient to fill the shape.

5 Adjust the settings for other options in any way you wish. Click OK.

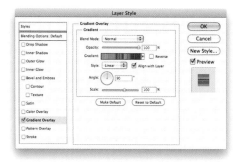

Or make sure the vector mask thumbnail is selected (as shown on page 164), then choose a "style" from the Options bar (also on page 164). Click the tiny triangle in the Styles panel to add even more options.

Manually change the path of a shape

You can change the outline of a vector shape at any time:

1   Click the vector mask thumbnail in the Layers panel.

2   Use the Direct Selection tool (the white arrow tool) and the Pen tools from the Tools panel to make changes to the shape's vector path:

 • **To display the points and curve handles,** single-click the path with the Direct Selection tool. Drag points to new positions and drag curve handles to modify curves.

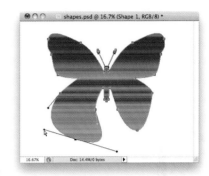

 • **To add additional points** to the path, click on the path with the Pen tool. (When the Pen tool is positioned over a segment of the path, it automatically changes to the Add Anchor Point tool.)

 • **To delete a point,** click an existing point with the Pen tool. (When the Pen tool is positioned over an existing point, it automatically changes to the Delete Anchor Point tool.)

 • **To change** an existing point from a smooth point to a corner point (or vice versa), click the point with the Convert Point tool.

Transform a vector shape

Apply any of the transform operations (see Chapter 4 for more details) to a vector shape.

1   Click the vector mask thumbnail in the Layers panel.

2   To transform the shape, do one of the following:

• From the Edit menu, choose "Free Transform Path," then drag the corner handles to scale or distort the shape.

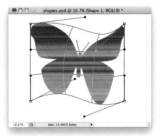

• From the Edit menu, choose "Transform Path," then choose one of the options in the submenu; drag the corners or handles. The example on the right uses the Warp option.

Stroke a vector shape with a brush

Although you can change the color fill of a vector shape over and over, a stroke (a border) you add to a shape must be rasterized. This means the stroke itself will not be attached to the vector shape, but will be automatically rasterized to a separate layer, where you can move it and modify it separately from the shape. You can also apply more than one type of stroke and each will be on its own layer.

1 Draw a vector shape: Choose the Custom Shape tool and select a form from the *Custom Shape picker,* as explained on page 164.

The shape is added to the **Layers panel** as a *Shape layer* (below, left). The layer consists of a color fill thumbnail and a vector mask thumbnail.

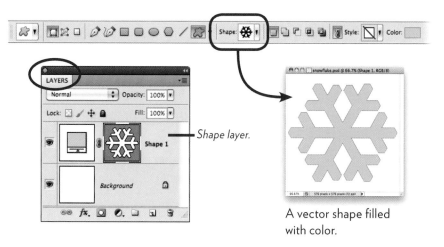

Shape layer.

A vector shape filled with color.

2 Open the **Paths panel.** Click the *Load path as a selection* button (below, left). The path in the main window turns into a *marching ants* selection (as shown below, right).

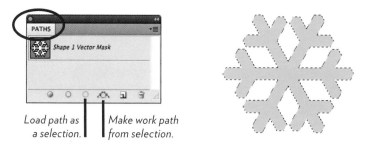

Load path as a selection. | Make work path from selection.

3 Still in the **Paths panel,** click the *Make work path from selection* button (above). You'll see a new *path* layer called "Work Path."

4 Back in the **Layers panel**, create a new layer *below* the *selected* Shape layer: Command-click (PC: Control-click) the *Create a new layer* button at the bottom of the panel (circled, below). *This layer is where the raster stroke will be created.* The vector object will thus be on one layer, and the raster stroke will be on another.

5 Select the Brush tool in the Tools panel.

6 Choose a brush type: Click the Brush Preset picker in the Options bar to select a brush style and size.

In the Options bar, set the opacity and flow both to 100%.

Choose a foreground color.

(*Or* in the Options bar, click the Tool Preset picker [the extreme left item in the Options bar], double-click one of the preset brushes to select it, then choose brush size, color, etc., as above.)

7 Make sure the **new layer** in the **Layers panel** is selected.

Make sure the **Work Path** layer is selected in the **Paths panel**.

8 At the bottom of the **Paths panel**, click the *Stroke path with brush* button (below, left).

Stroke path with brush.

The final brush stroke effect.

As you can see above, the new brush stroke is placed on the new layer as a rasterized image. You can modify its color and opacity just like any other pixel-based layer.

Paint with brushes

You'll use brushes to paint, retouch, alter colors, and basically do most of the work in Photoshop. A variety of tools other than paintbrushes are considered to be "brushes" in Photoshop: the Eraser, the Clone Stamp tool, the Blur, Sharpen, and Sponge tools, etc. Many tools, even if they don't apply paint, have brush characteristics assigned to them, such as brush tip shapes, sizes, hard or soft edges, opacity, etc. The following pages explain how to use and customize brushes and save them as presets for future use. It's important to experiment with this! Try different brush tips with the Blur tool when you want to smooth areas or soften edges, or give the Eraser an odd brush shape and create patterns with it. The possibilities are infinite (we're pretty sure).

The Brush Options bar

When you select the Brush tool from the Tools panel, the Options bar (below) changes to provide brush options and access to the Brush Presets (customized brushes already made for you) and the Brush panel.

Brush Preset picker.   *Painting mode.*   *Let tablet pressure control opacity.*   *Airbrush mode.*

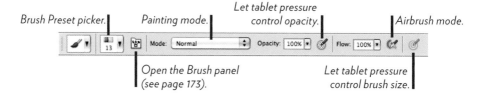

Open the Brush panel (see page 173).   *Let tablet pressure control brush size.*

- From the **Brush Preset picker** (shown below), adjust the *size* of the brush and its *hardness* (a soft edge is feathery; a hard edge is solid).

- Check out the other brush tips you can choose from this panel. You can paint grass, leaves, patterns, and much more. If you don't see extra brush tips, click the triangle in the upper-right corner and add more.

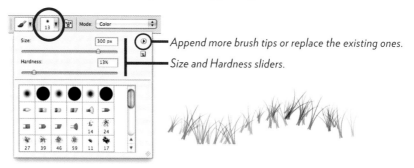

Append more brush tips or replace the existing ones.

Size and Hardness sliders.

To see previews of the kinds of brush strokes any brush will make, use the Brush panel, shown on page 173.

Select and use a brush

When you're ready to select and use a brush, follow these steps:

1 Select the Brush tool in the Tools panel.

2 Set a foreground color: Click the Foreground color swatch to choose a color from the Color Picker, *or* select a color from the Swatches panel. (See Chapter 11 for details about color.)

3 In the Options bar, click the Brush Preset picker to choose a brush tip, then set the brush *size* and *hardness.*

4 In the Options bar set the brush *opacity* and *flow.*
Opacity determines how transparent the color is;
flow affects how much paint is applied to the image.

5 Press-and-drag on your canvas. Voilà!

Change the cursor

In the Photoshop preferences, you can change the cursor according to your working preference. This is an **important thing to know** about any brush tip (Eraser, Clone, etc.), so spend a few minutes experimenting with the different cursors. Then when you're working with the various brush tools, you'll know what the options are for precise brush work.

The "Normal Brush Tip" displays a cursor that is the size of the portion of the brush stroke that has at least 50 percent opacity; this means if you have a soft brush where the edges are feathered, your cursor will show you just the center area of the brush stroke even though pixels are being affected outside that area. The "Full Size Brush Tip" displays the entire area affected by the brush stroke, so for a soft brush, it will be a large cursor.

• From the Photoshop menu, choose Preferences > Cursors.
(PC: Edit menu, choose Preferences > Cursors.)

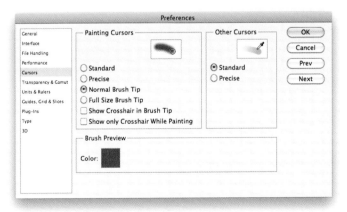

Resize brushes

Because so many tasks in Photoshop require frequent adjustments of the brush tools, it's helpful to know several different ways to change the brush size or hardness/feather on the fly.

- **To reduce the brush size**, tap the left bracket [on the keyboard.

- **To enlarge the brush size**, tap the right bracket].

- **To give the brush a softer edge**, press **Shift [**. This softens the brush by 25 percent with each tap of the bracket key.

- **To give the brush a harder edge**, press **Shift]**. This hardens the brush by 25 percent with each tap of the bracket key.

- **To interactively change brush size while working on an image**, press Control Option and drag *horizontally* (PC: press Alt and right-click; drag *horizontally*). The brush changes size as you drag so you can see how large or small it is, but it doesn't paint while you drag.

  Drag right to enlarge the brush (below, left). Drag left to reduce the brush size (below, left).

- **To interactively adjust the brush hardness setting**, press Control Option and drag *vertically* (PC: press Alt and right-click; drag *vertically*). The brush edge changes as you drag so you can see how hard or fuzzy it is, but it doesn't paint while you drag.

  Drag upward to create a softer edge (below, right). Drag downward to create a harder edge (below, right).

Drag horizontally to adjust brush size (see details above).

Drag vertically to adjust the hardness setting of the brush edges (see details above). The brush above has a very soft edge.

More customization with the Brush panel

The Brush panel and Brush Presets panel, shown below, are expanded versions of the Brush Preset picker (see page 170).

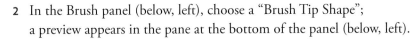

1   Make sure the Brush tool is selected in the Tools panel, then click the "Brush panel" button in the Options bar, *or* the panels Dock, *or* from the Window menu, choose "Brush."

2   In the Brush panel (below, left), choose a "Brush Tip Shape"; a preview appears in the pane at the bottom of the panel (below, left).

3   **To load other preset brush shapes,** click the "Brush Presets" button in the top-left corner of the Brush panel.

    In the Brush Presets panel that opens (shown below, right), click the panel menu icon in the top-right corner, then select another collection of presets. You might need to scroll down to see the new brushes if you *append* the new brushes instead of *replace* the existing brushes.

    Whatever you replace or append in the Brushes panel will appear in the Brush Presets picker in the Options bar, and vice versa.

The Brush panel.   **The Brush Presets panel.**

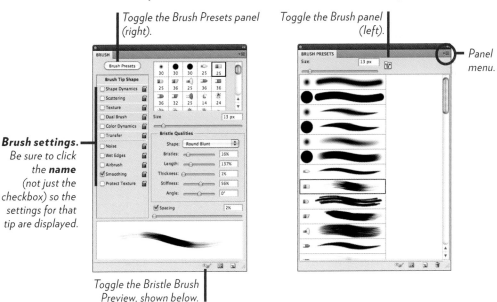

Toggle the Brush Presets panel (right).

Toggle the Brush panel (left).

Panel menu.

Brush settings.
Be sure to click the **name** (not just the checkbox) so the settings for that tip are displayed.

Toggle the Bristle Brush Preview, shown below.

When you choose a Bristle Brush (brushes whose icons are drawings of brush tips), the Bristle Brush Preview shows the angle and orientation of the stylus on a pressure-sensitive tablet, whether you have one attached or not.

Paint with a textured brush

Some of the brush presets already have a texture applied to them, but you can add texture or a pattern to any brush to create interesting strokes.

1   Select the Brush tool in the Tools panel.

2   In the Options bar, click the Brush panel icon: This opens the Brush panel, as shown below.

3   In the Brush panel, click "Texture" in the left column to display the texture controls on the right side of the panel. (Don't just check the box—make sure you *click on its name* to display the options.)

4   Click the texture/pattern swatch to reveal a pop-up panel of textures or patterns. Click one of the swatches to select it, *or* click the small triangle button to select from a list of other textures and patterns.

As you experiment with various settings, the preview updates to show the results of your brush modifications.

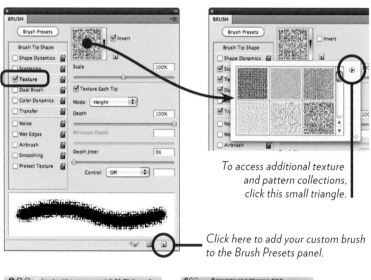

To access additional texture and pattern collections, click this small triangle.

Click here to add your custom brush to the Brush Presets panel.

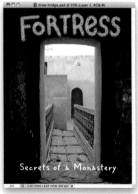

More about brush settings

The Brush panel provides more ways to modify a brush stroke than we'll ever need, but occasionally we find some obscure setting that is just exactly what we want. The options on the right side of the Brush panel apply to the brush characteristic or effect selected on the left side of the panel. Watch the preview pane at the bottom to see what you created.

Shape Dynamics are the dynamic elements of a brush that can be made to change during a brush stoke, such as size, color, or opacity.

Scattering sets the number and placement of marks that combine to make a brush stroke.

Texture uses patterns to add texture to a brush.

Dual Brush combines two brush tips to make one brush stroke. With a brush tip selected, click "Dual Brush," then select a second brush tip from the presets that appear on the right side of the panel.

Color Dynamics adjusts color variations of a stroke, based on current foreground and background colors. The "Fade" option sets the variation of colors as a specific number of steps.

Transfer determines how paint changes during a brush stroke. For instance, the "Fade" control looks at the paint opacity setting in the Options bar and fades it from there down to 0.

Noise adds noise (speckles) to soft brush tips that contain gray values.

Wet Edges simulates paint build-up along brush stroke edges.

Airbrush simulates soft, sprayed airbrush brush strokes.

Smoothing creates smoother brush strokes.

Protect Texture applies the same pattern and scale to all brush presets that have texture. To create a consistent texture, select this option when you paint with multiple textured brush tips.

Spacing is an option that's available on the right side of the Brush panel when "Brush Tip Shape" is selected at the top of the left column. Increase the Spacing value to add space between the basic elements of a brush tip and create "spacey" brush strokes.

The Mixer Brush

 The Mixer Brush is stored under the regular Brush tool in the Tools bar (press on the Brush tool icon to reveal the panel of other brushes).

The Mixer Brush simulates the way a physical paint brush handles color and reacts with color already on the paper. The Mixer Brush contains two paint *wells.* The first, the *reservoir well,* is loaded with the foreground color; the second, the *pickup well,* picks up paint from the canvas and mixes it with the reservoir color. The settings you apply determine exactly how the brush and canvas colors interact with each other.

The Mixer Brush Options bar

When the Mixer Brush is selected, the Options bar (as usual) changes to show brush-specific settings.

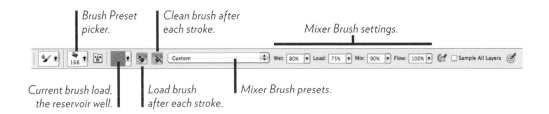

Brush Preset picker.

Clean brush after each stroke.

Mixer Brush settings.

Current brush load, the reservoir well.

Load brush after each stroke.

Mixer Brush presets.

- **Load or clean your brush:** The *Load brush after each stroke* button loads the color that was under the brush tip at the **end** of the previous stroke. The *Clean brush after each stroke* button loads the color that is under the brush tip at the **start** of the next brush stroke.

- **Current brush load:** Click the triangle next to the color swatch and choose "Load Brush" to load the foreground color. If you want to keep the foreground color loaded, click the *Load brush after each stroke.*

  Or choose "Clean Brush" to clear the brush of color.

- **Mixer Brush presets** menu: Dry, Moist, Wet, Very Wet, etc. To modify the chosen preset, use the controls to the right of that menu:

    Wet determines how much paint the Mixer Brush picks up from the canvas. A higher number makes longer brush streaks.

    Load specifies how much paint is loaded in the reservoir well. A lower number makes the brush stroke run out of paint more quickly.

    Mix determines how much foreground color is mixed in with the brush stroke. A low percentage adds more foreground color; a high percentage adds less foreground color and more canvas color.

    Flow determines how much paint is applied by the brush.

Create a painterly effect with the Mixer Brush

Choose a blank canvas, a color-filled layer, or an existing image to paint on, as in the example below. Then do the following:

1 Select the Mixer Brush (under the Brush tool).

2 Choose a brush from the Brush Presets picker.

3 In the Options bar shown on the opposite page, set the Mixer Brush options and settings. In most cases, click *Clean the brush after each stroke* button to keep from contaminating colors too much.

4 Drag the Mixer Brush in an image to paint.

A photo customized with the Mixer Brush.

Below are the Mixer Brush settings used for this painting. I chose the Mixer Brush preset called "Wet," then modified the settings on the right (Wet, Load, and Mix).

If you choose to paint on an image, duplicate the image layer and work on the duplicate to preserve the original. You can paint on the duplicate and easily make new duplicates from the original as you experiment with various brush settings.

Brush Blending Modes

When you paint with a brush, you can choose a brush **blending mode** to alter how the brush color interacts with other colors in the image.

These blending modes are exactly like the Layer Blending Modes explained on page 98; instead of using a Brush blending mode, you can place brush strokes on separate layers, then apply a Layer Blending Mode.

However, the Brush Blending Mode includes two options that aren't available on Layers: *Behind* and *Clear*. *Behind* paints only on transparent areas of a layer, as shown below, giving the appearance of "painting behind" existing pixels on the layer. *Clear* paints transparency (which means it erases, just like the Eraser tool).

1 Select the Brush tool in the Tools panel.

2 In the Options bar, select a blending mode from the "Mode" pop-up menu. The samples of various blending modes below shows how different modes affect the brush stroke and the image. The effects differ depending on the color and value of the brush stroke as well as the underlying image.

3 Select a foreground color and paint on a layer.

Normal.   *Screen.*   *Difference.*   *Divide.*

*The **Behind** Brush Blending Mode paints only on transparent pixels. This black brush stroke is actually on the same layer as the hand and wine glass. (Keep in mind, though, that you have more options if you paint the brush stroke on another layer.)*

Paint with the Clone Stamp tool

The Clone Stamp tool can resolve many of your retouching challenges—it's more versatile than many users realize. At its most basic level, you simply select a part of an image as a *source,* and then paint that source onto another area of the image (see page 58). But you can also scale or rotate from the source, and even paint part of an image from one document onto an image in another document. You can set up to five separate sources and switch between them as needed.

To adjust the clone options in the Clone Source panel, open this panel from the Window menu.

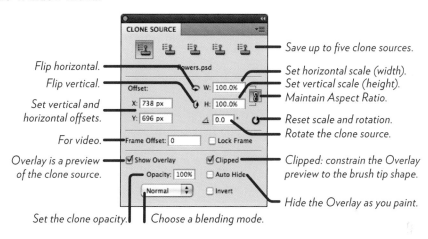

Save up to five clone sources.

Flip horizontal.
Flip vertical.

Set vertical and horizontal offsets.

Set horizontal scale (width).
Set vertical scale (height).
Maintain Aspect Ratio.

Reset scale and rotation.
Rotate the clone source.

For video.

Overlay is a preview of the clone source.

Clipped: constrain the Overlay preview to the brush tip shape.

Hide the Overlay as you paint.

Set the clone opacity. | Choose a blending mode.

A simple clone project

Paint elements from one photo into another photo using the Clone Stamp.

1 Open two photos (both photos must be in the same color mode, either RGB or CMYK). Separate them so they are not in the single tab (drag the title bar of one photo away from the tab until it separates).

Original flower photo.

Original dog photo.

— continued

2 Select the Clone Stamp tool.

 3 In the Options bar, click the Brush panel icon. In the Brush panel, choose a brush tip, set opacity, flow, and blending mode.

 4 In the Options bar, click the Clone Source panel icon. In the Clone Source panel (shown on the previous page), choose from these behaviors for the cloned image you paint:

- Flip the cloned image horizontally or vertically.
- Adjust the scale of the cloned image.
- Rotate the cloned image as you paint.
- Adjust the opacity of the cloned image.
- Choose a blending mode for the cloned image.
- Choose to "Show Overlay" (so the brush displays what you're going to paint before you actually commit to it) and clip it to the brush tip shape (select the "Clipped" option).

5 In the Options bar (shown below):

- From the "Sample" pop-up menu in the Options bar, choose which layers to sample.
- Make sure the Mode is "Normal" (unless you choose otherwise).
- Select or deselect "Aligned" (see below).

Select "Aligned" to make the Clone tool remember the brush tip position at the end of your last stroke, and continue from there when you start the next brush stroke. When "Aligned" is deselected, each brush stroke starts at the original position of the selected clone source.

6 Set a clone source: Position the Clone Stamp brush tool over a part of the image you want to clone somewhere else, then Option-click (PC: Alt-click).

First, position the Clone Stamp tool here and Option-click (or Alt-click) to set a clone source.

Next, position the Clone Stamp tool somewhere else; press-and-drag to paint.

To set additional clone sources, first select one of the other clone source icons in the Clone Source pane, then Option-click or Alt-click on the portion of the image you want to clone.

7 With a clone source selected, position the Clone Stamp tool in the image where you want to start painting, then drag to paint.

With a black background and the Clone brush hardness set to 0% (a very soft-edged brush), painting near the edge of existing flowers creates the illusion of new flowers disappearing into the shadows of other flowers.

8 **To use the other Photoshop document as a clone source,** Option-click (or Alt-click) in the document where you want to set a clone source. In the example below, I opened a photo of Robin's dog, Rosetta, and Option-clicked in her face.

Next, position the Clone tool in the window where you want to start painting with the new clone source; press-and-drag to paint.

A large, soft-edged Clone Stamp brush creates a soft transition between the original flower image and the clone source, which is Robin's dog from another open Photoshop document.

TIP: For some projects, you might want to make a selection of the area in which you intend to work so the rest of the image is protected.

Paint with the Gradient tool

The Gradient tool creates smooth blends between colors. You can use a gradient to fill a layer or a selection. Apply different blending modes and adjust gradient opacity to create unique effects. Choose from a collection of preset gradients, create your own, or modify existing presets to fit your needs.

Fill a layer or a selection with a preset gradient

1   Select the Gradient tool in the Tools panel.

2   In the Options bar, click the triangle button (on the right side of the Gradient swatch, shown below) to open the Gradient picker, then choose one of the preset gradients.

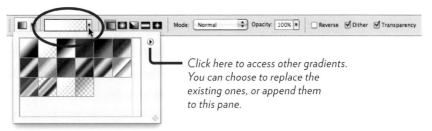

Click here to access other gradients.
You can choose to replace the
existing ones, or append them
to this pane.

3   In the Options bar, select one of the **gradient style** buttons:

Linear gradient: Blends colors in a straight line.

Radial gradient: Blends colors in a circular shape.

Angle gradient: Blends colors in a counter-clockwise sweep around the starting point.

Reflected gradient: Creates a linear gradient on each side of the starting point.

Diamond gradient: Blends colors in a diamond shape. The starting point (the first click/press of the Gradient tool) is the center of the diamond. The gradient ending point (the release of the Gradient tool) sets the corner of the diamond shape.

4   In the Options bar (below), make the following settings:

• Choose a **blending mode** from the "Mode" pop-up menu, and set the gradient **opacity**.

Or if you prefer (and **we recommend**), leave the Mode set to "Normal" and opacity at 100%. **Create a new layer** for the gradient and make sure the new layer is directly above the photo. Keep in mind that the gradient layer will affect *all* layers beneath it; if you want the gradient to affect just the one layer below, clip the two together (see pages 106–107).

- Check "Reverse" if you want to reverse the color order.
- Check "Dither" if you want smoother blends and less color banding (usually a good idea).
- Check "Transparency" to preserve any transparency that's included in the gradient. Deselect for an opaque gradient.

5   Paint the gradient: Position the Gradient tool where you want to start, then press-and-drag to a point where you want to end the gradient (below left). If you don't like the result, **Undo** (choose Edit > Undo) and try again.

If you applied the gradient **directly to the photo** (instead of on a separate layer), you cannot change the gradient—you must undo and try again.

If the gradient is **on its own layer** (below right), adjust the opacity and blending mode in the Layers panel for that selected layer. You can always throw away the layer and start over.

Starting point.

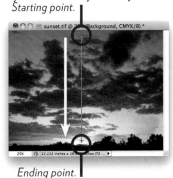

Ending point.

The gradient, applied to a new layer.

To cycle through the modes, select the Move tool, hold down the Shift key, and press + (plus) or – (minus).

"Color Burn" layer blending mode results.

Paint with a pattern

The Pattern Stamp tool paints with a pattern. Select a pattern from the pattern libraries or create your own.

A layer beneath the Moon layer is painted with the Pattern Stamp tool.

Rasterized text painted with the Pattern Stamp tool.

Below is one example—experiment with all the options!

1 Select the Pattern Stamp tool.

2 Choose a brush from the Brush Presets panel in the Options bar. In the example above-left, I chose a round brush with 0% hardness.

3 Set mode and opacity options in the Options bar. Above, the mode is *Divide* and the opacity is *45%*.

4 Select "Aligned" in the Options bar if you want to maintain the continuity of the pattern, no matter where you start the brush. *Or* deselect "Aligned" if you want to restart the pattern at a new start point when you stop and start painting again.

5 Click the Pattern swatch in the Options bar to select a pattern, as shown below. To load additional patterns, click the small triangle button (circled).

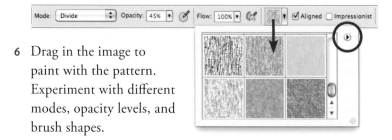

6 Drag in the image to paint with the pattern. Experiment with different modes, opacity levels, and brush shapes.

Color Tools

Photoshop's color creation and selection tools are enough to make design survivors from the pre-digital world weep with joy. When we first saw the Eyedropper tool in Photoshop 1.0, we said, "Even if that's all it does, I gotta have it." Now we can work with color in a variety of fun and powerful ways.

Photoshop's color tools enable you to select from color swatches, create custom colors, select color from an image, select a color library from an impressive list of libraries, create your own custom color library, match colors between images, and exchange color libraries with InDesign and Illustrator. There's even a special Kuler™ panel for downloading color libraries from the Internet (see page 190).

In this chapter we cover the basic tools and operations you should know to create, select, and apply color in your documents.

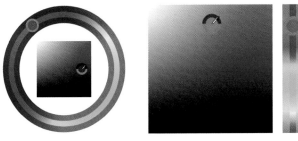

The HUD color picker is just one of the color selection tools you can use. On the left is the Hue Strip version of the color picker; on the right is the Hue Strip version (seep page 188).

Pick a color

Whether you want to fill a shape or layer, change the color of type, or fill a brush with a specific hue, use one of these methods to pick a color.

The Color panel

Colors you create in the Color panel are temporary, as opposed to colors in the Swatches palette (pages 190–191) that you can use again and again.

To open the Color panel, from the Window menu, choose "Color."

• The Color panel has **Foreground** and **Background** boxes, just as in the Tools panel. Often it is critical that you recognize which box is chosen, so look carefully at the illustrations below.

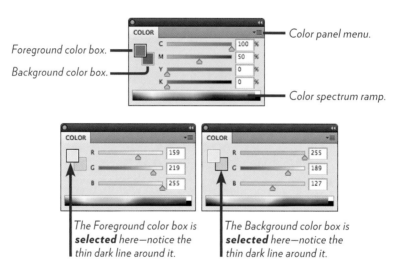

Foreground color box.

Background color box.

Color panel menu.

Color spectrum ramp.

The Foreground color box is *selected* here—notice the thin dark line around it.

The Background color box is *selected* here—notice the thin dark line around it.

To create a color in the Color panel, do one of the following:

Single-click in the color spectrum at the bottom of the panel.

Or drag the color sliders to set a value for each hue.

Or type a value in the text box for each hue.

IMPORTANT: If the Background color box is selected, it can affect color choices with other tools! If you ever use a keyboard shortcut expecting, say, the Foreground color box in the Tools panel to change color, but it changes the Background color box instead, that's because the Background color box in this Colors panel is selected. It's really annoying. Get in the habit of tapping the D key to make sure the Foreground color box in the Color panel is selected.

To change color modes and spectrum:

To create CMYK colors or RGB colors, open the panel menu (shown below) and choose the color sliders you need.

To ensure that you don't create colors out of the proper **gamut**, make sure the spectrum matches the slider mode, as shown below.

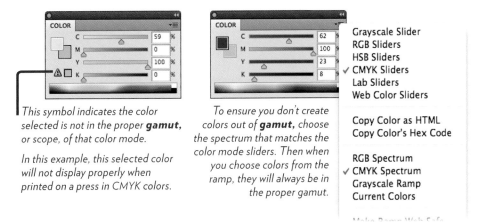

Grayscale Slider
RGB Sliders
HSB Sliders
✓ CMYK Sliders
Lab Sliders
Web Color Sliders

Copy Color as HTML
Copy Color's Hex Code

RGB Spectrum
✓ CMYK Spectrum
Grayscale Ramp
Current Colors

This symbol indicates the color selected is not in the proper gamut, or scope, of that color mode.

In this example, this selected color will not display properly when printed on a press in CMYK colors.

To ensure you don't create colors out of gamut, choose the spectrum that matches the color mode sliders. Then when you choose colors from the ramp, they will always be in the proper gamut.

The Adobe Color Picker

The Adobe Color Picker is one of two main tools for color.

1   To open the Color Picker, click the Foreground or Background color box in the Tools panel.

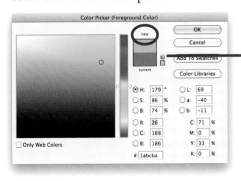

This symbol means the new color is not "web safe," meaning the color you've chosen might not display exactly like this on old monitors.

2   Single-click in the vertical color spectrum to choose a hue and display its variations in the large preview pane on the left. Then click in the preview pane to choose a shade or tint of the hue; your chosen color appears in the "new" preview box.

3   Click "Add to Swatches" to add that particular color to the Swatches panel, where you can easily access it at any time.

4   Click OK to place that color in the color box (Foreground or Background) that you had selected.

The HUD color picker

You can use the HUD (Heads-Up-Display) color picker to select a color on the fly when any painting tool is selected.

The HUD color picker is available in two types: the Hue Wheel (below, left) and the Hue Strip (below, right). It is your own personal preference which one to use. **To change the type of HUD color picker:**

1 From the Photoshop menu, choose Preferences > General (PC: From the Edit menu, choose Preferences > Performance).

2 From the "HUD Color Picker" pop-up menu, choose one of the Hue Wheel or Hue Strip options.

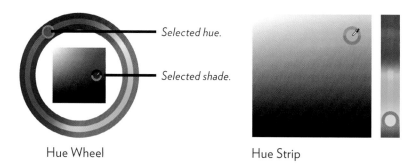

Hue Wheel   Hue Strip

To use the HUD color picker:

1 Press Control Option Command (PC: Shift Alt right-click) and hold down the cursor in the center of the image area. The HUD Color Picker appears. Let go of the modifier keys, but continue to press down.

2 Still pressing down, drag the circular selection shape to the outer ring of the Hue Wheel or to the vertical bar in the Hue Strip; drag around or up and down to select a color hue.

3 Still pressing down, drag the selection shape back to the square and select a shade or tint of the color hue. The top-right corner represents pure color.

4 Release the cursor. The Hue Wheel or Strip disappears and the selected color appears in the Foreground color box of the Tools panel and in your brush.

The Eyedropper tool

Pick a color with the Eyedropper tool—it samples (picks up) the color from the pixel in which you click.

- To select a **foreground** color with the Eyedropper tool, single-click a color in the image.

- To select a **background** color with the Eyedropper tool, Option-click (PC: Alt-click) a color in an image.

You can choose whether or not to display a **sampling ring** (the large circle shown in the image below) when you use the Eyedropper. This is a handy way to see exactly which pixel color you will pick up.

1 Choose the Eyedropper tool; check "Show Sampling Ring" in the Options bar.

2 **In the Color panel**, click the foreground or background color, depending on which one you want to load color into.

3 Press-and-drag the Eyedropper on the image and the sampling ring appears. Inside the ring, the top half-ring of color is the current color selection in the pixel sampled by the Eyedropper; as you move the Eyedropper around the image, that color changes. The bottom half-ring is the previous color selection.

When the top half displays a color you want, click and that color is loaded into the foreground or background (whichever you chose).

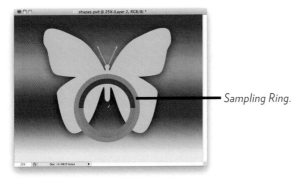

Sampling Ring.

TIP: You can invoke the Eyedropper sampling ring on the fly while you're painting with a brush: Make sure the Foreground color swatch is selected in the Color panel (not the Tool panel), and make sure "Show Sampling Ring" is chosen as in Step 2, above. While painting, Option-click (PC: Alt-click) on the image to get the Eyedropper sampling ring. Let go, and your brush is loaded with the new color.

The Kuler™ panel

When you open the Kuler panel, it connects via the Internet to collections of color themes created by an online community of designers and artists. If you're not confident in your color sensibilities or in choosing color combinations that go well together, you'll find lots of different color themes that professional designers have created for you.

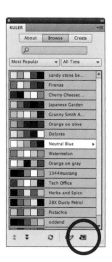

1   Open the Kuler panel: From the Window menu, choose Extensions > Kuler.

2   Click the "Browse" button at the top of the panel to display the color selections.

You can use the pop-up menus to select color themes by category (Most Popular, Highest Rated, etc.), or by date.

3   To add a color theme to your Swatches panel, select the theme, then click the *Add selected theme to swatches* button at the bottom of the panel (circled, right).

Manage the Swatches panel

The Swatches panel keeps project colors accessible and organized. You can share swatches with other people and other applications.

To open the Swatches panel, from the Window menu, choose Swatches.

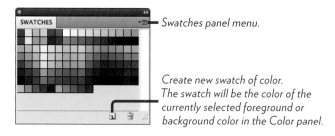

Swatches panel menu.

Create new swatch of color. The swatch will be the color of the currently selected foreground or background color in the Color panel.

Add a color to the Swatches panel

In the Color panel (not the Tools panel), select a foreground color, then click the "New Swatch" button at the bottom of the Swatches panel. *Or* create a foreground color in the Color panel, click an empty space in the Swatches panel, name the color, and click ok.

Delete a color from the Swatches panel

Drag a swatch to the panel's Trash icon (you won't see the grabber hand until you actually *press and drag* the swatch).

Save a custom set of swatches as a library

From the Swatches panel menu, choose "Save Swatches…" then choose a location. This creates a .aco file for Photoshop (an **Adobe** color file format for color swatches).

Share swatches with InDesign and Illustrator

1   In the Swatches panel, create color swatches you want and delete swatches you don't want to include.

2   From the Swatches panel menu, choose "Save Swatches For Exchange…." This creates a .ase file (Adobe swatch exchange file format).

Robin Swatches.ase

3   Choose a location in which to save the swatches file— you can save it anywhere.

4   Load the file into the Swatches panel of InDesign or Illustrator: From that application's Swatches panel, choose "Load Swatches," then select the .ase file you created.

Load or replace color libraries

From the Swatches panel menu, choose "Load Swatches," "Replace Swatches," or choose one of the color library names in the panel menu. You can choose to append (add) the swatches, or replace the existing ones.

Reset the default swatches library

From the Swatches panel menu, choose "Reset Swatches."

Match color

You sometimes have to work with photos that have different color casts. If the photos are supposed to look similar, the different casts can be distracting or look amateurish.

Instead of experimenting with settings for Hue/Saturation and Color Balance, try Photoshop's Match Color feature.

1   Open both images in Photoshop, then choose the *target* image, the image you want to adjust (make it the active window).

2   From the Images menu, choose Adjustments > Match Color.

3   In the "Match Color" dialog, select the *other* image, the one you want to match *to,* in the "Source" pop-up menu.

4   Check the "Preview" box to see the effect on the target image.

5   To reduce the effect, use the "Fade" slider. If necessary, adjust the other sliders.

6   Click OK.

Source image.   Target image.   Modified target image.

• In multilayered files, you can choose the layer you want to adjust.

• To base the color adjustment on specific color areas in the source image, make a selection in the source image, then check "Use Selection in Source to Calculate Colors."

• To apply the color adjustment to only a part of the target image, check "Use Selection in Target to Calculate Adjustment."

• Choose "Save Statistics" to apply these adjustments to future images.

• You can "Load Statistics" from other sources (a friend or coworker).

12 Filters & Effects

Filters can alter an image's appearance in many ways. Using filters, you can transform your images with textures, special effects, artistic effects, distortion, blurs of various kinds, sharpness, lens corrections, lighting effects, and much more. The possibilities are dizzying, especially when you consider that most filters provide many adjustment options.

Before you apply a filter to a layer, you can first convert the layer into a Smart Object layer. When you apply a filter to a Smart Object layer, the filter becomes a Smart Filter, a non-destructive editing layer that preserves the original image. When you use Smart Filters, you can modify filter settings (or disable the filter) at any time after you've applied them. It's a very smart and efficient way to work.

These are just a few of the filters available that can add visual interest to your project.

Filter Gallery

Some filters can only be applied to RGB files, so if the filter you want to use won't work because your image is in CMYK mode, go to the Image menu and choose Mode > RGB Color. Also, keep in mind that an image's resolution can affect the appearance of some filter's results—a higher resolution usually produces a more refined result. We often increase an image's resolution before we apply certain filters, then reduce the resolution (see page 70).

To use the filters and effects from the Filter Gallery:

1 Select a layer in the Layers panel to which you want to apply a filter or an effect. *Or* make a selection in a layer.

2 From the Filter menu, choose "Filter Gallery." The dialog opens, shown below, with the selected layer content in the preview pane.

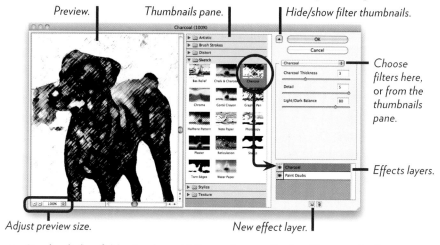

Preview. *Thumbnails pane.* *Hide/show filter thumbnails.*

Choose filters here, or from the thumbnails pane.

Effects layers.

Adjust preview size. *New effect layer.*

3 Single-click a folder in the middle section to display filters and effects.

4 Select one of the filter thumbnails (such as "Charcoal," shown above).

5 With a filter/effect thumbnail selected, adjust the settings on the right side of the dialog. The filter is added to the *effects layers* list in the bottom-right corner. Each filter you choose will *replace* the existing one in the list until you click the *New effect layer* button, then it gets added and the effects affect each other.

   • Add as many effects as you want.

   • Click the eyeball icon to turn the effect on or off.

   • The stacking order of effects layers can affect the image results, so drag a filter up or down in the list to try different combinations.

6 Click OK. Once you click OK, *those effects are permanently applied* (see Chapter 7 about the History palette if you made a mistake!).

Filters in the Filter menu

You can also choose and apply filters from the Filter menu. Some of these same filters are in the Filter Gallery, in which case Photoshop automatically opens them in the Filter Gallery dialog (shown on the opposite page) when you select one of them.

There are too many filters to show them all here. Experiment with each one so you know what the possibilities are.

A sampling of filters from the Filter Gallery.

Glowing Edges.   Poster Edges.   Grain Vertical.   Torn Edges.

Artistic filters

The **Artistic** filters create painterly effects. Some effects that may not immediately appeal to you with their default settings can look very different when you experiment with the adjustment sliders. The *Watercolor* filter is shown on the left.

Blur filters

There are several different types of blur filters. The most commonly used is the *Gaussian Blur* to slightly soften the image. Another favorite is *Surface Blur,* which attempts to keep edges sharp while blurring between edges; use it to improve a low-resolution image that has lots of noise and graininess, as shown below.

Original image.   Surface Blur applied.

Brush Stroke filters

The **Brush Stroke** filters create a painterly or graphic look, using different brush stroke effects. By adjusting the filter sliders, a wide variety of beautiful effects are possible. The *Accented Edges* filter is shown to the left.

Noise filters

Noise is random or orderly color or grayscale pixels that can be used to create texture, add visual interest, and cover up problem areas, such as uneven color or dust specs. The *Reduce Noise* filter smooths areas of color that contain noise, yet preserves edges. In the example to the left, I used *Add Noise.*

Pixelate filters

The **Pixelate** filters can simulate halftone patterns or translate images into blocks of color or different kinds of dot patterns, such as the *Mezzotint* filter, shown below-left, and the *Mosaic* filter, below-right. (There is a completely different *Mosaic Tiles* filter under **Texture.**)

Render filters

The **Render** filters create cloud patterns and simulated light reflections. They are also useful with 3D techniques, which we don't cover in this book.

This *Lens Flare* filter simulates the flares that different types of camera lenses create.

This *Lighting Effects* filter simulates various types of lighting. You can add drama, focus, or visual interest to a portrait, a landscape, or just about any subject when you apply lighting effects. It's another creative option that you can take advantage of in Photoshop.

Sharpen filters

Unsharp Mask and *Smart Sharpen* are the most effective filters in this category. *Unsharp Mask* (left) adjusts the contrast of edge detail. *Smart Sharpen* provides more control, letting you set the amount of sharpening separately for shadows and highlights.

Sketch filters

The **Sketch** filters add texture and create a fine art or hand-drawn look. Many of the filters, such as the *Stamp* filter shown here, use the current foreground and background colors.

197

Filters and Smart Objects

Smart Object layers contain image *data,* but not the actual *image.* This allows non-destructive editing, which means the original image on that layer is preserved and can always be recovered. Once a layer is a Smart Object, any filters you apply are automatically Smart Filters, which are perpetually adjustable and non-destructive.

To convert a regular or Background layer to a Smart Object, select the layer, then:

- From the Layer menu, choose Smart Objects > Convert to Smart Object. *Or* from the Filter menu, choose "Convert for Smart Filters."

  Both commands do the same thing; they convert the *selected* layer into a Smart Object, preparing it to accept filters as Smart Filters.

To make changes to the original image on a Smart Object layer, double-click the Smart Object thumbnail. The original image opens in a separate window. Make the changes, save them in the original location, then close the original's window. The edited image is now visible in the Smart Object layer.

Work on a low-res version of a Smart Object

If a project requires large, high-resolution images—which can cause slower performance on your computer, especially when applying certain filters—you can work with low-resolution versions of the images as Smart Objects and apply Smart Filters and adjustments, then later replace the low-res versions with the high-res images. Any transformations, filters, warping, and effects you created are applied to the high-resolution replacement images.

1 Select a Smart Object, then from the Layer menu, choose Smart Objects > Replace Contents.

2 In the "Place" window that opens, choose the high-res version of the image, then click "Place."

3 Click OK. The new content is placed in the Smart Object.

Remember, however, that a filter applied to low-res image might have a more intense result than the same filter applied to a high-res image.

The Accented Edges filter applied to a low-resolution image (left) and a high-resolution image (right).

Copy a filter to another Smart Object

Instead of going through the steps necessary to apply the same filter to another layer or multiple layers, **copy filter effects** from one Smart Object layer to another Smart Object layer.

- Option-drag (PC: Alt-click) the filter effects icon on a Smart Layer and drop it onto another Smart Layer (shown below).

This is the effects icon on a Smart Layer, being dragged to the Smart Layer above.

Delete or disable a Smart Filter

To delete a Smart Filter, do one of the following:

- In the Layers panel, right-click on the Smart Filter name (the filter name, *not* the layer name), then choose "Delete Smart Filter."

- *Or* drag the individual Smart Filter layer to the Trash icon at the bottom of the Layers panel.

To disable a Smart Filter, do one of the following:

- In the Layers panel, right-click on the Smart Filter name, (the filter name, *not* the layer name), then choose "Disable Smart Filter."

- *Or* in the Layers panel, click the Eyeball icon next to the Filter Mask thumbnail (which will delete all the Smart Filters in that collection) or next to an individual Smart Filter name.

TIP: The first item in the Filter menu shows the most recent filter applied.

- If you choose the recent filter that appears as the first item in the Filter menu, it **applies the same filter settings** as the last time it was used.

- As a shortcut **to open the filter dialog**, Option-click (PC: Alt-click) the recent filter name at the top of the Filter menu (which is the last filter you used). This opens the filter dialog so you can modify the settings, instead of applying the filter with the previous settings.

Lens Correction

Two types of lens distortion are common with cameras: *Barrel distortion* (straight lines bow out toward the edges, like a barrel) and *Pincushion distortion* (straight lines bend inward toward the center). The Lens Correction filter corrects both types, and more.

1 Open an image that needs correction (usually something with straight lines), then from the Filter menu, choose "Lens Correction...."

The original image with lens distortion.

Remove barrel or pincushion distortion.

Correct vertical or horizontal perspective.

Show a grid to help with alignment.

2   In the "Auto Correction" pane, you can choose the camera model and lens type that you used to shoot the photo, and let the default settings take care of correcting the image.

3   If you don't know the camera information, click the "Custom" tab.

    In the "Geometric Distortion" section, drag the "Remove Distortion" slider toward the *barrel distortion* icon (left) or toward the *pincushion distortion* icon (right).

4   If necessary, in the "Transform" section, drag the "Vertical Perspective" and the "Horizontal Perspective" sliders left or right. The icon at either end of the sliders indicates the effect that slider will have on the image.

5   When the corrections are made, click OK.

The corrected image.

The Liquify filter

The Liquify filter distorts and warps raster images. It's a great filter for retouching, or for special effects, because it creates substantial distortion with minimal quality degradation.

1   Select a layer, *or* make a selection of part of a layer.

2   From the Filter menu, choose "Liquify...."

 3   In the Liquify dialog, use the Freeze Mask tool to "paint" areas of the image that you don't want to change. This is only necessary if your brush size overlaps areas that you don't want to affect.

    To erase the Freeze Mask when you're done, use the Thaw Mask tool.

4   Choose one of the liquify tools from the panel on the left side, then drag in the preview pane to distort the image. I used the Forward Warp tool in the example below.

5   Use the Reconstruct tool from the Tool panel to paint the changes back to normal, *or* click the "Reconstruct" button on the right side to undo the liquify effects step by step, *or* click "Restore All" to undo all distortions at once. Click OK when you're happy with it.

Brush Density sets the feathering (softness) of the brush. The edge of a softer brush (lower number) does not impact the image as much as a hard edge.

Brush Pressure sets the impact of distortion when you *drag* a tool in the preview area. Low settings have less impact per drag.

Brush Rate and **Turbulent Jitter** set the speed of distortions when you hold a tool *stationary* in the preview area. Drag just a wee bit, then hold the tool still.

See page 41 for another example of how to use this filter for retouching.

Experiment with the various tools and settings.

To make the brush larger, press **]**.

To make the brush smaller, press **[**.

Vanishing Point

Vanishing Point lets you create a perspective plane mesh on top of an image. When you retouch or clone on top of the perspective plane, the edits are scaled and oriented to the plane in perspective. For instance, you might want to extend a brick patio into the background of a photo, or cover the side of a house with wood planks. Vanishing Point enables you do that, in perspective. To keep the perspective plane information in a document (to use later), save the document in PSD, TIFF, or JPEG format.

The example shown below just barely scratches the surface of what can be done in Vanishing Point, but it demonstrates how this feature can overcome certain complex retouching challenges.

Clone an image with Vanishing Point

1 Open an image that has a perspective in it, such as a long walkway or a building. To protect the original, create a new layer to work on.

2 From the Filter menu, choose "Vanishing Point...."

3 In the Vanishing Point dialog that opens, use the Create Plane tool (selected by default) to click in the preview area and set the four

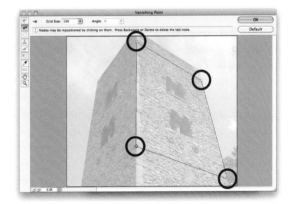

corners of a rectangle that will define the perspective plane surface. The opacity of the image below is lightened so you can see the perspective plane clearly (right).

To add a plane, select the Create Plane tool and drag the existing plane's edge away from the plane (shown on the right). By default, new planes are drawn at a ninety-degree angle to the source plane.

Anything painted, cloned, or pasted onto a plane adheres to that plane's perspective.

—continued

In this example, we want to *clone* the sides of the tower, in perspective, to make it taller.

4 Select the Edit Plane tool. Drag the top edge of the front plane upward to extend the perspective. Repeat for any other edge necessary to cover your intended work area (below).

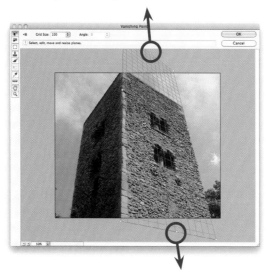

5 To protect other parts of the image from being altered, select the Rectangular Marquee tool, then double-click inside the front plane to select it.

6 Choose the Clone Stamp tool. Option-click (PC: Alt-click) on the image (a window in this example) to set a clone source. Position the brush where you want to put another window, then drag in the image, creating another window; repeat as necessary. No matter where on the plane you paint, the cloned image maintains the correct perspective.

• You can paste an item into the "Vanishing Point" dialog window to create a *floating selection,* which conforms to the perspective of any plane that it's dragged into. You can scale, rotate, flip, or move a floating selection.

7 Click OK when finished.

13 Camera Raw

Many of today's cameras can be set to shoot photos in what is called *Camera Raw.* Raw is not a format itself, but refers to a myriad of camera-specific formats that capture *uncompressed* image data, retaining much more color and luminance information than other formats, such as TIFF or JPEG. With raw photos you can manipulate and adjust images in ways not possible with compressed formats.

While some adjustments in Camera Raw, such as noise reduction and lens correction, are also available in Photoshop's Filter menu, the Camera Raw method provides more control, preserves the original, and allows you to store the adjustments separately.

Many of the Camera Raw adjustments in Photoshop work not only with raw photos, but also with JPEG and TIFF formats. Some of the original data in JPEGs and TIFFs, however, is deleted in the camera during the compression process, so some adustments have limitations.

There are several different raw formats; in the unlikely event that you need to work with images in a format that is not supported by Photoshop, visit the Adobe web site and search for "DNG Converter." The DNG (Digital Negative) Converter converts other raw formats to the DNG format, which is compatible with Photoshop and other Adobe applications.

Open an image in Camera Raw

Open an image in Camera Raw by doing any one of the following:

- In Photoshop, from the File menu, choose "Open…."
  In the Open dialog box, single-click to select an image.
  From the "Format" menu at the bottom of the dialog box,
  choose "Camera Raw," then click "Open." The image opens
  in the *Camera Raw* interface.

- If the Applications bar is visible in Photoshop, click the
  Bridge icon 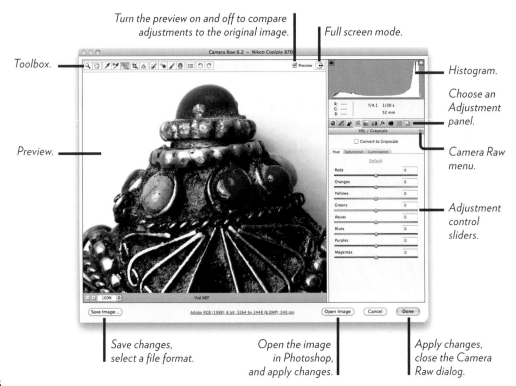 to open the Bridge application.
  Select a photo, then click the *Open in Camera Raw* icon
  in the Options bar. It opens in the *Camera Raw* interface.

- Double-click a raw image anywhere on your computer. Raw
  images have filename extensions such as .NEF .DNG, .RAW,
  .CRW and .CR2. They open in the *Camera Raw* interface.

The Camera Raw interface

The main elements of the Camera Raw interface include a large preview,
a tool panel located just above the preview, and a pane on the right that
displays the controls for the currently selected Adjustment panel.

Turn the preview on and off to compare adjustments to the original image.

Full screen mode.

Toolbox.

Histogram.

Choose an Adjustment panel.

Preview.

Camera Raw menu.

Adjustment control sliders.

Save changes, select a file format.

Open the image in Photoshop, and apply changes.

Apply changes, close the Camera Raw dialog.

The Camera Raw Adjustments panels

To display a specific Adjustment panel, click its button in the row of buttons (shown below) that are located below the Histogram (shown on the previous page). Hover the cursor over an icon to show a tool tip description of the item; click an icon to display its controls. Some specific examples and exercises are on the following pages, but spend some time experimenting.

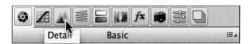

The toolbox

The toolbox provides a collection of tools for editing the image in the preview.

Zoom tool: Enlarge or reduce the preview.

Hand tool: Drag in the preview area to reposition an enlarged image.

White Balance tool: Click on a tonal value in the preview to adjust the image's white balance. (We usually simply select "As Shot" or "Auto" from the "White Balance" pop-up menu.)

Color Sampler: Click colors in the preview to show their RGB values in a list. You can list the values of up to four colors.

Target Adjustment tool: Hold down this tool icon to reveal a pop-up menu, then choose the type of adjustment you want to make. Click on the preview to sample a range of pixels, then drag horizontally to modify the pixels that fall within the sampled range. See page 210 for an example.

Crop tool: Crop the image.

Straighten tool: Press and drag to align the drawn line with a feature in the image that you want to straighten horizontally or vertically.

Spot Removal tool: From the "Type" pop-up menu, choose "Heal" or "Clone," then set the brush size *(Radius)* and opacity.

Red Eye Removal tool: Adjust the *Pupil Size* slider and the *Darken* slider (if necessary), then drag a rectangle that covers the entire eye and part of the face. The tool will only remove the red color.

Adjustment Brush tool: Paint effects on the image that can be adjusted after you apply them. See page 211 for an example.

Graduated Filter: Place one or more gradations over an image to affect exposure, brightness, contrast, saturation, clarity, sharpness, or color.

Noise Reduction

Unless a camera is set to shoot in a raw (uncompressed) format, a photo will have some degree of compression applied to it in the camera, which creates *noise*. Noise appears as unwanted texture, artifacts, and odd-colored pixels in the image. The example below shows an image that was originally scanned at a low resolution and saved as a JPEG. We can fix that.

1 Open an image in Camera Raw (see page 206).

2 In the Camera Raw dialog, single-click the "Detail" icon.

3 In the "Noise Reduction" section, give *Luminance* a high setting, and give *Luminance Detail* a low setting. See the example below.

4 In the "Noise Reduction" section, drag the *Color* slider to the right to remove color noise. Drag the *Color Detail* slider to the right to recover edge detail, if necessary.

5 Drag the *Luminance Contrast* slider right to enhance edge contrast.

6 **Save the file** in one of the following ways:

• Click "Save Image…" to save your adjustments; choose a file format and location in which to store the image.

• Click "Open Image" to apply the adjustments and open the image per usual in Photoshop.

• Click "Done" to apply the adjustments and close the Camera Raw dialog box.

Before Noise Reduction.

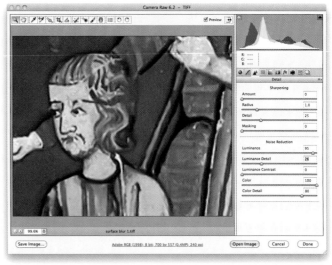

After Noise Reduction.

Lens Correction

Use Camera Raw's Lens Correction tools to fix common lens distortions such as barrel and pincushion distortion. Also use these tools to fix the even more common vertical or horizontal distortion, as shown in the example below.

1 Open an image in Camera Raw (see page 206).

 2 In the Camera Raw dialog, click the "Lens Corrections" icon.

3 In the Lens Corrections panel that opens, make sure you've got the Zoom or Hand tool selected. Click the "Manual" tab. Based on the type of distortions you need to correct, drag the adjustment sliders in the "Transform" section. Watch the preview to see the result.

In this example, I adjusted the *Vertical* slider to straighten the door frame, then adjusted the *Rotate* slider a bit for a straighter appearance.

To reset all the settings, hold down the Option key (PC: Alt key), and the Cancel button turns into a Reset button.

4 Save the file as described in Step 6 on the opposite page.

Before Lens Corrections.

After Lens Corrections.

Option-click (Alt-click) the Cancel button to reset all the controls.

The Targeted Adjustment tool

The Targeted Adjustment tool samples a range of pixels at the point where you click in the preview, then modifies pixels that fall in that range as you drag the tool horizontally across the preview. In the example below, we want to change the color of the building, but retain the realistic color changes between light and shadow areas (a perfect example for when this tool is invaluable).

1 Open an image in Camera Raw (see page 206).

 2 *Press* on the Targeted Adjustment tool in the Tools panel to display its tool menu (shown below-right); select the type of settings you want to adjust.

> **Hue:** Adjust the colors.
>
> **Parametric Curve:** Adjust highlights, lights, darks, and shadows.
>
> **Saturation:** Adjust the saturation of the color range you click on.
>
> **Luminance:** Adjust the brightness of the color range you click on.
>
> **Grayscale Mix:** Convert the image to grayscale and adjust the grayscale values of the color range you click on.

3 Press on a color in the preview that you want to adjust, then drag the Adjustment tool left or right in the preview to adjust the hue of the sampled pixels. You'll see the sliders on the right adjust as you drag.

4 Save the file as described in Step 6 on page 208.

The initial click samples a range of pixels that will be modified.

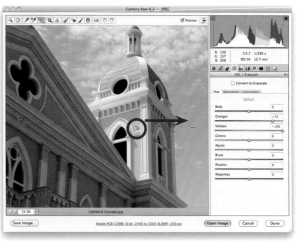

Press and drag the tool left or right in the preview to modify the selected settings (the Hue, in this example).

The Adjustment Brush

Use the Adjustment brush to paint individual areas of an image and adjust them separately. This unique brush enables you alter your image by painting with exposure, contrast, clarity, and other adjustments.

1 Open an image in Camera Raw (see page 206).

2 Click the Adjustment Brush icon in the Tools panel.
In the lower pane on the right, adjust the brush settings
(Size, Feather, Flow, and *Density).*

3 Check the *Auto Mask* button so the brush will detect edges and keep the brush effect confined to specific areas. If the effect spills over into an unwanted area, select *Erase* and paint out the spill-over.

4 Adjust the sliders to settings you want to paint with. Don't worry about precise settings—modify them *after* you paint them in.

5 Paint on the preview image. A *Pin* appears in the painted area to indicate an adjustment; additional brush strokes are added to the same group (the *Add* button is selected by default). To paint a different area, which sets another Pin, click *New.*

   To see areas where you've painted with an Adjustment Brush, hover the brush over a Pin.

   To adjust the image, click on a Pin to select it, then adjust the sliders.

6 Save the file as described in Step 6 on page 208.

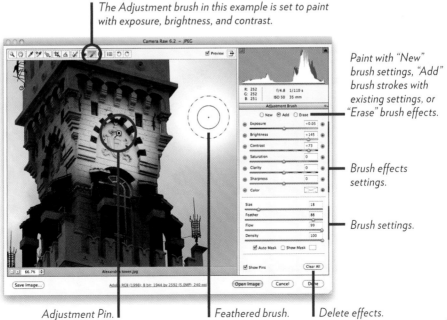

The Adjustment brush in this example is set to paint with exposure, brightness, and contrast.

Paint with "New" brush settings, "Add" brush strokes with existing settings, or "Erase" brush effects.

Brush effects settings.

Brush settings.

Adjustment Pin.　　Feathered brush.　　Delete effects.

Camera Raw images as Smart Objects

To place a raw file in a Photoshop document as a Smart Object, from the File menu, choose "Place." Select a raw image file, then click "Place." See pages 111–113 about working with Smart Objects.

Overexposure warning

When adjusting *exposure* or *brightness* in Camera Raw, you can enable a *highlight clipping warning* that will highlight overexposed areas as red. A *shadow clipping warning* will highlight shadows that are too dense for a printer to duplicate as blue. You can see the warning effects, below-left.

To turn the warnings on or off, click the triangles at the top left and right corners of the histogram in the Camera Raw dialog (below-right).

Shadow clipping warning button (left) and highlight clipping warning button (right).

Red and blue clipping warnings.

14 Puppet Warp

Puppet Warp is a distortion tool that provides an amazing amount of control in manipulating an image. You can literally treat images or objects on a layer (*not* a Background layer) like a puppet and bend them to suit your needs. You can protect areas from being affected by the warp, and you can even overlap parts of an image on top of another part of the same image, as in the example shown below (on the right).

Puppet Warp is useful not only for radical warping, as shown below, but also for all sorts of retouching projects, such as shaping the folds of a blouse, modifying a hair style, trimming a few inches from a waistline, etc. Use this warping technique to fix camera distortions, create unusual effects, or enhance a smile.

Elements on a transparent layer, such as the sock puppet below, are especially easy to manipulate since they have no background distortion to deal with.

The original image.

Puppet Warp applied to the image.

Puppet Warp an image on a transparent layer

If the image you plan to warp is on a Background layer, double-click the layer (and click OK) to convert it to a regular layer. The image in this example is on a transparent layer by itself, *above* a Background layer filled with white. If you want to separate an individual element from an image, see pages 158–163 on how to use the Pen tool to create a Path around an object, then delete everything else on the layer.

1   Open an image and select the layer you want to warp.

2   From the Edit menu, choose "Puppet Warp" (if it's not available, you've probably got the Background layer selected).

3   In the Options bar (shown below), adjust the following settings:

> **Mode:** Choose *Distort* for a highly elastic mesh.
>
> **Density** (spacing of mesh points): Choose *Normal* for now. *More points* increases precision, but can slow down processing time.
>
> **Expansion** (expands or contracts the outer edge of the mesh): Expanding the mesh on a transparent layer such as this can help prevent hard edges. Try *2 px* for now.
>
> **Show Mesh** (toggles the mesh visibility): The mesh (as shown below, right) doesn't have to be visible to use Puppet Warp.

4   Click on the image to add "pins" to areas you *don't* want to move and also add pins to areas that you *do* want to move.

> When a pin is *not selected* (when it's a solid yellow color), it doesn't move and thus protects the area around it.
>
> When a pin is *selected,* a black dot appears in the center of the pin, and you can drag it and its surrounding area to another position.

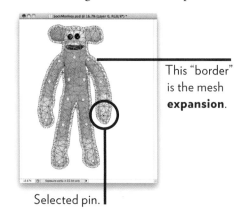

This "border" is the mesh **expansion**.

The original image.   Selected pin.

5 Select a pin (press on it) and drag it to warp the mesh, as shown below, left. If parts of the image move that shouldn't, Undo (choose Edit > Undo), then add pins to the area that you need to anchor.

To delete a selected pin, press Delete.

To delete a pin that is not selected, Option-click the pin (PC: Alt-click).

To remove all pins, click the *Remove all pins* icon in the Options bar.

To select and move multiple pins at once, Shift-click to select them, then let go of the Shift key and drag to move.

To rotate the mesh around a selected pin, Option-press on a pin (PC: Alt-press). When a circle appears around the selected pin, drag to rotate the mesh.

6 **To commit the transformation**, click the *Commit Puppet Warp* icon (the checkmark) ✔ in the Options bar, *or* press Enter. Photoshop won't let you do anything else outside the Puppet Warp until you commit to it, and it won't save the points for you.

Overlap mesh areas

If you have a floating image on a transparent background, you can move a mesh area in front or behind another mesh area: Select one pin, then click one of the *Pin Depth* buttons in the Options bar.

Set pin forward and *Set pin backward* buttons.

Set pin forward.　　Set pin backward.

215

Puppet Warp a Smart Object

To make sure you **leave the original image intact**, before you proceed with Puppet Warp, convert its layer to a Smart Object:

1 Select the layer you plan to warp.

2 From the Layer menu, choose Smart Objects > Convert to Smart Object.

You might want to edit the original image in a non-warp way, yet have those changes appear in your Puppet Warp. **To edit the original Smart Object** image after you've applied Puppet Warp:

1 Commit the Puppet Warp adjustment: Press Enter or Return.

2 Double-click the Smart Object layer thumbnail. The original, unwarped version of the image opens in a new edit window.

3 Make edits, then Save. Close the new edit window.

Warped Smart Object.   Warped and edited Smart Object.   Unharmed original.

Puppet Warp anything

Puppet Warp isn't just for puppets—it's a powerful tool for reshaping any image. In the example below, the pins placed around the edges serve as anchors to keep those areas pinned down as other areas are warped.

The photo above-left is not distorted, it's just a house with lots of character. Puppet Warp, above-right, makes it look more stable for online buyers.

Index